# PLANTING FOOD PLOTS

## FOR DEER & OTHER WILDLIFE

# OUTDOORSMAN'S EDGE®

### THE ULTIMATE GUIDE TO

# PLANTING
# FOOD PLOTS
## FOR DEER & OTHER WILDLIFE

*By*
*John Weiss*

Front Cover image courtesy: Mossy Oak/BioLogic
Back Cover photos: Fiduccia Enterprises and Jay Cassell
Inside Images and Illustrations by John Weiss unless otherwise indicated

Published by: Woods N' Water Inc.
Peter and Kate Fiduccia
P.O. Box 65
Bellvale, NY  10912

Printed in the United States of America
10  9  8  7  6  5  4  3  2  1

ISBN: 0-9707493-4-1

# TABLE OF CONTENTS

# INTRODUCTION

The late Earl Nightingale, one of the nation's foremost radio broadcasters, once related a story that serves as an ideal foundation for this book. Seems one day a country pastor was driving down a rural road in his parish when he rounded a curve and spotted a beautiful whitetail buck feeding in a lush alfalfa meadow. A little farther along, a turkey gobbler suddenly flew across the road ahead of him. Eventually the pastor came to a farmhouse that was a sight to behold Leading up to the home was a neatly manicured gravel driveway that was bordered by a fence that glistened with fresh paint. The house itself literally sparkled with cleanliness and just outside its kitchen window lay an impressive vegetable garden anyone would be proud of. In the yard surrounding the home, beautiful flower beds and shade trees completed the idyllic setting. The minister then spotted the farmer on his tractor in a nearby field, turning the earth with almost perfectly aligned furrows. Other nearby fields had already been planted and were thriving with corn, oats and wheat. The pastor sat in his car along the side of the road, waiting for the farmer to complete his plowing-turn and begin coming back in the opposite direction. When the farmer saw the pastor, he shut down his tractor, walked over and the two shook hands. "The Lord certainly has blessed you with a fine and beautiful place," the minister remarked. "Yes He has," the farmer replied. "But you should have seen this place when He had it all to Himself." This true anecdote nicely sets the stage for the focus of this book and what you, too, can accomplish in terms of land-improvement practices designed to enhance deer and other wildlife populations. A great many sportsmen either own a modest amount of acreage, or lease land, or have a relative who possesses property, or have a close friendship with someone who owns land, and as a result of any of these situations the sportsman has almost sole use of the property for hunting, wildlife photography or other recreational purposes. In some instances the property may be quite large, while in other cases the amount of acreage may be relatively small. But one thing all these sportsmen and landowners have in common is that they'd like to see more wildlife on the property, particularly whitetail bucks sporting big antlers. However, as all farmers are well aware, Mother Nature is capricious. She's not a kind, benevolent caretaker of her land and its inhabitants. She's a harsh old witch who doles out only the minimum needed for her flora and fauna to barely survive. Furthermore, as diligent and hard-working as they may be, state and federal wildlife agencies typically do not have the manpower and other resources to intensively manage either public or private land bases to their fullest wildlife potential. Enter the hunter-sportsman who, if he's willing to invest the effort and become a steward of the land, is able to turn even spartan habitat into a wildlife paradise and, more specifically, a mecca of trophy deer. However, in this book we won't pull any punches by implying that wildlife management is easy and can be undertaken on a whim or with only a sporadic, half-hearted mindset. The unvarnished truth is that the effort requires continual but usually brief periods of hard physical labor, not to mention regular doses of research time and planning. In the latter regard, we'll list available (and mostly free) reference sources and agencies that can be consulted for technical information that's beyond the scope of this book. Throughout this book's many chapters we'll also list sources for seed, planting stock, artificial feeding devices, vitamin and mineral supplements designed for wildlife, and companies that offer equipment specific to the wildlife manager's needs. Moreover, all the while it's important to keep in mind that habitat changes rarely occur overnight. Understandably, in our fast-paced world we sometimes tend to become impatient and discouraged when improvements don't take place in a New York minute. So it's necessary to be realistic in our expectations and accept the fact that we cannot rush the natural order of habitat transformation. Many changes we enact may take weeks and months to become barely noticeable, and some may take years. But time passes quickly and one's rewards steadily become more and more evident, generating a growing satisfaction that the steward's ongoing investments of time, work and money are well-worthwhile. Notice we haven't emphasized the need to own or have exclusive access to a huge amount of land because even the smallest acreage can be improved upon to attract and hold more deer and numerous other wildlife species. This is because the three-legged stool that supports all wildlife is food, water, and cover. So clearly, if your 50 acres provides all three of these essentials in abundance and, meanwhile, the larger parcels comprising hundreds of acres of land surrounding your's are wildlife wastelands, guess where the deer and other game and non-game species are going to rivet their attention and call home? Another thing we won't emphasize is the need to invest a king's ransom in expensive agricultural land or high-priced equipment. There is indeed an axiom that always holds true—buy the best you can afford—but transforming a modest amount of marginal quality acreage into attractive wildlife habitat is not the same as attempting to earn a living by farming. The deer couldn't care less if you ride a small, used tractor and the rows in your one-acre corn food plot are not perfectly straight. Nor will the deer give a whit if your half-acre food plots in designer clover-blends or other forages are a bit "weedy." Moreover, the pheasants and quail may actually prefer your small-grain food plots to have patchy bare ground here and there so they can simultaneously feed and scratch for grit. And that brushy area that a farmer would otherwise want to clear away for still another agricultural crop can be looked upon by you as an ideal place to be easily and quickly improved upon to provide ideal turkey nesting cover or a windbreak for deer seeking shelter from the weather's assault. So what are you waiting for? In a few short years, the splendid buck hanging over your fireplace mantle, the wafting aroma of the wild turkey roasting in your oven, and the sights and sounds of ducks and geese winging overhead will be testimony enough that your work afield was worth every minute.

—*John Weiss*

# CHAPTER 1

## FINDING YOUR OWN
## HUNTING PARADISE

There are several different types of situations in which food plots for deer, and other wildlife management efforts, are given birth.

• You may already own rural property and simply want to begin making it more attractive to deer and other game and non-game species.

• You may be interested in purchasing a modest parcel of land with a home on it that you can move into and begin enjoying year-around country living while gradually over the years greatly improving its hunting and other recreational potential.

• You may be interested in purchasing rural property but not have any interest in leaving the city to live in the country. Rather, you'd simply like to manage the land for wildlife and perhaps build a cabin on the acreage for seasonal use.

• You may want to consider leasing acreage either by yourself or perhaps with several other family members or regular hunting partners and during the term of the lease improve the wildlife habitat.

• A final possibility is a rent-to-own option. This occurs when a landowner wants to sell his property but is willing to rent it during the meanwhile and, if the renter eventually decides he wants to buy the land, the accumulated rental fees he's been paying for several years are credited toward the purchase price.

In any of these situations, the "where factor" will have a crucial influence on the cost of the property if you're a buyer or the lease fee if you plan to be a renter.

Whether you want to own the property outright, or just lease it, its location also will dictate the availability of utility services, their initial installation costs if not already in place, and their monthly service charges.

There also may be property tax implications and perhaps insurance considerations, especially if the land is purchased.

I know one landowner who initially purchased 400 acres 20 years ago. It's close to a large city that is mushrooming in size and this has caused his property to rapidly increase in value. That's the good news. The bad news is that it also means a steep upward spiral in his property taxes every year, forcing him to periodically sell

There are many land-acquisition options available to the prospective wildlife manager. Over the long term, buying the property is the most expensive but also the most satisfying.

off a portion of his land to developers in order to pay the taxes; consequently, the 400 acres he once owned has slowly but systematically shriveled to only 130 acres.

I also know another individual who bought 100 acres close to a rural high school. When he built a pond on his arid land, to serve as a place for deer to drink and to attract waterfowl, his liability insurance rate quadrupled. His agent explained that, in building the pond, he had created an "attractive nuisance" among local kids tempted to sneak in to fish or skinny dip and if one of them ever drowned he'd be on the sour end of a devastating lawsuit. So at the outset, one's budgetary situation plays a key role and nearly all other elements are secondary.

The "people factor" is equally important in another regard. Your employment circumstances will have a telling influence upon where you and your significant other may choose to acquire land, as will the various needs of any children or other immediate family members who may be in the picture.

Yet in all of these scenarios, there are several rules of thumb that will help pave the way to your intended wildlife management program on your own place.

First, keep in mind that if you intend to own the property and live upon it, you'll have to commute to work each day. So generally, this means looking at tracts of land no more than 40 miles distant from your place of employment. That's 80 miles of round-trip driving per day. This travel time is important because commuting from a rural area into a city invariably takes longer than commuting an equal distance from a suburban neighborhood; although metropolitan traffic may be gridlocked at times, it's seldom as slow-going as when driving narrow, winding county roads that haven't yet in the early morning been cleared of snow and ice.

If you don't plan to actually live on the land but intend to simply buy it to manage for wildlife and enjoy other recreational pursuits, you'll similarly want it to be located within a 40 mile drive so that you can visit the property often, quickly and easily. In short, no matter how attractive a given property may be, it's not worth your serious investigation for the purposes of managing its wildlife habitat if it's located such an uncomfortably long distance from where you live and work that it can be visited and tended only on an infrequent basis.

Strive to find a property that has multiple uses and is within convenient driving distance of where you work. For some, other factors such as schools and health care may also be important.

3

Leasing a property also involves a myriad of circumstances. Again, you and your partners will want the land to be within a reasonable driving distance. And since putting in food plots and instituting other wildlife management practices take time, you'll want nothing less than a five-year lease. Moreover, you'll want full permission (in writing) from the landowner to plant and rotate wildlife forages, engage in forestland management, do periodic maintenance work such as road grading and gate installation, and to have full legal authority to restrict access by others.

In leasing a property, another critical ingredient is not only your own living and employment circumstances but also those of your lease partners. If a potential lease partner has a job history of being regularly transferred to another region every few years, or has a unique employment schedule such as working the night shift and sleeping all day, or doesn't have the financial ability to share equally in the many aspects of leasing a property and planting food plots, or is averse to physical labor, problems with him will continually hamper the efforts of the other lease participants and strain their patience.

## HOW TO BEGIN YOUR SEARCH

Once you've mentally committed to owning or leasing a tract of land, then commit yourself to a full year of time to locate and thoroughly investigate the many properties that will present themselves for consideration. Twelve months may seem like a long time but you'll be investing a good amount of money and may conceivably be involved with that particular piece of property for the rest of your life, so you'll want to avoid mistakes you'll forever regret. Moreover, there will be many "drive-bys" and "talk sessions" that will enter the picture and consume time.

When my friend "Jim" committed to buying his own land, but not living on it, at least not immediately, he first took the rather unscientific but sound approach of simply laying out a roadmap. Then, using the map's scale and a pen, he drew a 40-mile-diameter circle around his home and then another circle surrounding his intended long-term place of employment. Then he considered properties only in that area where the two circles overlapped.

Jim now had established his reasonable driving limit from his home to the combination hunting/wildlife management land he wanted to begin looking for. He also had simultaneously established the comfortable driving distance to and from the land to his place of employment so that if he eventually began living full-time on his country place he wouldn't have an unbearably long commute.

An aerial photo helps narrow the search because the lay of the land determines its price. Prime agricultural bottomland is the most expensive, and hardscrabble ridge land is the least expensive. Something in between is perfect for the individual who wants to put in food plots and manage for deer.

It's a sensible approach, but also be sure to include in this picture the needs of other family members, such as the employment circumstances of a significant other, local schools for kids, medical care facilities and the like.

After researching the subject, Jim decided he needed a bare minimum of 50 acres for he and his adult son to hunt upon and manage for deer but at current local land prices he could afford up to a maximum of 100 acres. Right from the beginning he eliminated from consideration prime agricultural bottomland costing five-times as much as upland ground (gently rolling terrain) in the same region; after all, he didn't intend to farm for a living. But he also eliminated highland ground (steep, rocky ridgeland and hard-scrabble) because he was indeed going to put in assorted small plantings to "farm" deer. Jim figured those factors would significantly narrow his search, and they did.

Next, Jim placed a brief classified ad in the largest local newspaper, indicating his desire to buy vacant land, and at the same time began studying the for-sale listings placed by current landowners. He also made contact with a local realtor, expressing his interest; making contact with just one local realtor is sufficient because nowadays most of them in any given region work on a co-op basis in which they share listings.

Another friend, "Tom," offered the following bits of insight and cautioned against certain types of land-purchase considerations.

Foremost, he strongly advises against the seemingly logical idea of buying land bordering a National Forest or other public holding. He initially thought he could save plenty by buying just a small, 15-acre parcel of land that would give him his own place and yet additionally give him close, adjacent proximity to thousands of acres of other land to roam at will.

What Tom didn't take into consideration is that 15 acres is too small to establish diverse food plots and other meaningful wildlife management programs. Moreover, he found himself eternally plagued with trespassers during hunting season and poachers during the other months of the year. "Beginning on opening day of the deer season the traffic on my township road became horrendous. Hunters even parked along the road right in front of my house and walked through my backyard to get onto the national forestland. With that, my deer management efforts, which were marginal to begin with, went right down the tubes."

Another friend, "Matt," had a similar, disappointing experience he likewise didn't expect when he purchased 150 acres.

"My property is entirely surrounded on all sides by much larger privately owned farms," he explained. "So in those circumstances, I thought at first I could be successful putting in food plots and doing other things to manage for trophy bucks. Wrong! I eventually learned the owners of those farms, and their adult children and friends, intensely hunted deer and they shot at every target of opportunity . . . even button bucks. Since a whitetail has an average home-range of two miles, almost everything I've done to promote trophy deer production on my own place has ended up with young, immature bucks going into my neighbors' freezers."

Still another acquaintance, "Ned," wisely took what's probably the ideal-type in a land acquisition. "I live in deer-hunting heaven," Ned responded. "My 130 acres of land is bordered on one side by a wide river that cannot easily be crossed and on two other sides by a patrolled one-thousand-acre refuge where hunting is strictly prohibited. My home is on the fourth side. Since the refuge has vast areas of heavy bedding cover but little in the way of prime forage, deer flock to the nutritious food plots on my own land like ants to a picnic and as a result live to maturity and grow trophy antlers."

Finally, another hunter, "Morris," claims his hunting and wildlife-photography land is likewise a dream-come-true.

He told me, "It's 200 acres, surrounded on all sides by similar-size tracts

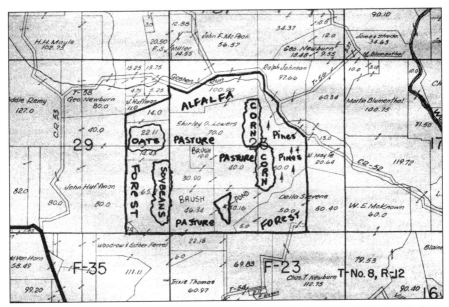

A county plat map reveals the names of property owners, the dimensions of their properties, and the amount of acreage in each parcel. Such maps are invaluable when making initial "drive-bys" to visually look over properties listed for sale.

of posted land where only the owners and their immediate families hunt. But they're all involved in a cooperative QDM program in which they're managing their properties for wildlife production and trophy deer. Since they all love to eat venison, they achieve a three-fold goal. They fill their freezers mostly with does, which keeps their herd sex-ratios in balance while at the same time allows the majority of young bucks to grow to maturity." (***Author's note:*** See the Quality Deer Management chapter at the end of this book)

## HOW TO EVALUATE A PROPERTY TO BUY OR LEASE

With several prospective tracts of land under consideration, next acquire a county road map, which reveals all the various rural routes in the region; these county and township roads are rarely shown on statewide roadmaps. You'll also need a plat map, which reveals the names of all the property owners and shows the amount and configuration of acreage each controls. Both of these maps can be obtained for little or no cost at the courthouse in the county where you plan to begin looking for your own place.

Next comes the matter of doing so-called drive-bys to visually take a look at the properties you've seen advertised, or know are available after talking with a realtor, or those which are in response to your own newspaper classified ads. The best time of year to engage in drive-bys is not during the summer when thick foliage hides everything from view. Instead, do your drive-by scouting in the late fall after the leaf-drop or in the spring before green-up, with an eye peeled for a diversity of cover types and terrain; look for a widely varied combination of heavy brush cover, mixed-aged stands of timber, former croplands, meadows now dormant, and plenty of edges and other irregular configurations. If you can't see much from the road, which is often the case in regions of very flat terrain, go to your county SWCD (Soil & Water Conservation District) or NRCS (Natural Resource Conservation Service) office and study an aerial photograph of the property in question.

With perhaps eight or ten different tracts of land you've scoped out and know you'd be perfectly satisfied to own or lease, now is the time to begin making face-to-face landowner contacts. If the result of a given landowner contact is encouraging, the final step (literally), before a sale or lease negotiation begins, is to do a walk-around of the property, preferably with a map and notepad in hand and the landowner by your side to answer questions.

Just a few of the things you'll want to learn from the landowner, which are sure to influence your decision-making process, are the following: The predominating soil types on the property; the types of crops/forages that

NORTHCOUNTRY WHITETAILS

**When considering buying or leasing land, the per-acre price is just one consideration. Will you have to hire a contractor to build access roads and install utilities? And what about local property taxes and insurance?**

have been previously and successfully grown on that acreage; the types (species) and amounts of native ground cover, hardwood trees, mast trees, fruitwood trees, and softwood trees on the property; what type and quantity of water is present (river, streams, ponds, springs, wells) and are they stable year-around water sources or only intermittent or seasonal; are there any high-security equipment/ storage buildings; are there interior access roads and/or equipment trails, where are they located, and are they all-weather or strictly seasonal; what utility services (electricity,

Once a property has been acquired, posting it is important, especially if the land has been vacant a long time and become subjected to heavy local use.

natural gas, propane, phone) are present or conveniently available and at what cost; is the immediate vicinity regularly patrolled by the county game warden and/or other local law enforcement personnel.

Regarding the leasing of upland ground, as this is being written, lease fees range from as little as $1 per acre per year to as high as $50 per acre, with the nationwide average being $3 per acre for hunting privileges alone and $25 per acre for food plot establishment and hunting privileges. The wide differential of course depends upon the quality of the land, how restricted the access to that land is, the land's inhabiting wildlife populations, and the propensity of the deer in particular to grow to trophy proportions in that specific region. Unless price is no object, the larger and most expensive properties are nearly always leased by groups of hunters rather than individuals.

As might be expected, there are many things an individual or small group, and the landowner, should agree upon in the signing of a lease. As mentioned earlier, the time and investment involved in planting food plots demands that a lease be for a minimum of five years, and you or your party should be guaranteed exclusive use of the property. But also, where on the property are you permitted to put in such food plots? Where on the property are you permitted to drive vehicles and operate field equipment, and which areas are restricted?

Where are you allowed to pitch a tent camp or park recreational vehicles such as pick-up campers? Is there a small cabin on the property you can rent for an additional modest fee? Can you selectively cut trees for habitat management? Should accumulated trash from your regular visits be bagged and taken home, or does the landowner have his own dumping site or a regular trash collection service which can be used?

Finally, everyone named in the lease agreement should sign and date the contract; then delegate someone to make photocopies for each participant's own records.

If the land is not going to be leased but bought outright, and you now have ownership of it, the very first order of business is to post it. Of course it's always a wise policy to be friendly with your surrounding landowner neighbors. And you may even agree upon occasion to give hunting permission to others who have the respect and courtesy to ask. But at the same time, especially if the property has been vacant for a long while before you purchased it, you'll want to protect your own interests by giving public notice that a new owner is now in charge and he will not tolerate anyone roaming upon the land at will.

# CHAPTER 2

## MAKE THE LAND
# PAY ITS OWN WAY

It's been said that, as a long-term commitment, buying land is the best thing anyone can invest in, simply because they're not making any more of it. But on a short-term basis, the new owner of raw land (that which is completely undeveloped in any way) who wants it to serve a variety of uses other than casual outdoor recreation will need to make improvements and thus will incur many expenses beyond the initial purchase price. If not already present, he'll need prepared places to park and store equipment, and interior trails or roads to access other areas of the property. He'll likely need utility services and perhaps eventually even want a home for a family to live in or at least a cabin for brief, periodic visits. Along with all of this will come property taxes and insurance.

Every parcel of land contains hidden treasures that, when harvested, improve the wildlife habitat and generate a cash-flow to finance many projects the landowner may want to undertake.

As the next order of

business, the land manager will undoubtedly want to begin improving the so-called "idle acres" on his property, and the most common way of accomplishing this is by transforming areas growing up in weeds into tree and plant growth that will better benefit man and beast alike.

In looking more specifically at increasing the deer and wildlife populations, and improving their habitat, a wide variety of still other expenses must be borne. We'll assume the landowner is not wealthy and therefore must be somewhat frugal in how much he's willing or able to invest in his wildlife habitat management and the creation of food plots, supplemental feeding programs, mineral licks, and myriad other projects.

The good news is that any given parcel of land holds many hidden treasures that, in a manner of speaking, can be "harvested" and in so doing will benefit deer and wildlife while at the same time generating a cash-flow that will go a long way toward financing other wildlife habitat projects.

## LET'S FIRST LOOK AT TREES

Contrary to the beliefs of many who are not trained in wildlife ecology, those expansive tracts of mature, high-canopy forestland we commonly see while driving cross-country are, for the most part, like barren deserts to all wildlife except squirrels and songbirds. Their browse (tender twigs, leaves and buds that wildlife feed upon) simply is too high and out of reach of ground-dwelling creatures. Furthermore, their broad crowns shade-out the understory and prevent the growth of ground-cover that otherwise would provide both food and shelter for many creatures.

By periodically—and selectively—removing a small percentage of these mature trees here and there, several benefits occur. Suddenly, in those previously shaded locations, profuse amounts of daily sunlight is able to bathe the forest floor and within a few brief

Mature forestlands are wildlife deserts. When a logging company selectively opens small areas, and sunlight can now bathe the forest floor, ground-level habitat is instantly improved.

1 2

months a cornucopia of ground-level plantlife springs up and attracts many game and non-game species because the immediate vicinity now provides them with a wide variety of feeding opportunities. This new, regenerative growth also provides cover needed by wildlife for hiding, resting and rearing their young. Equally important, the removal of a quantity of trees every year generates income which the land-owner can then reinvest in still other land-improvement projects. But before any cutting is done, planning is essential to a successful end result.

Opening up small forested areas creates ideal, future food plot sites where the land manager can plant still better wildlife forages than what nature provides on her own.

NORTHCOUNTRY WHITETAILS

I suggest first consulting with a forester associated with your state department of natural resources. Part of his job description is to work with private landowners, usually at no charge, in the area of what's called TSI, meaning timber-stand improvement. The process typically begins with a landowner making an appointment with a forester to actually "walk the property" to survey the standing timber and, in accordance with the landowner's wildlife management intentions, decide which trees have saleable value and should be removed and which should be allowed to remain. The forester at this time may even apply a small, spray-painted "blaze" on trees to be removed, or mark them with brightly colored flagging ribbon. At this time, in accordance with standard TSI practices, the forester will probably also want to mark for removal so-called "junkwood" trees of all ages and species that never will have any commercial or wildlife value.

If a state forester is not available for this work, private forestry professionals are available for a fee; ask your state-forestry department for their recommended listing of individuals. I give my highest praise to these private foresters because logging operations can involve many implications that can be very costly to the landowner in terms of his periodic timber sales and the long-term ecological health of his forestland. A trained forester looks out for the best interests of the forestland but also that of the landowner by acting on his behalf in negotiating the contract with a logging company and then overseeing the logging operation itself.

With trees marked for removal, the next step usually sees representatives from several logging companies invited to evaluate the trees for sale and submit bids. Such bids usually are quite competitive because they're mathematically calculated in accordance with the species of trees, their ages and therefore the number

NORTHCOUNTRY WHITETAILS

**Always consult with a trained forester who can mark trees for removal while leaving a diverse mix that best benefits the forest ecosystem.**

of board feet of lumber each tree will yield, and the lumber's current market value.

Since the bids will probably be very close, a more important consideration is "how" the trees are removed. Frankly, some companies are more harsh with the terrain than others and leave behind erosion-prone equipment ruts on skid trails and haul roads. Some minor damage is inevitable, especially in steep terrain that is difficult to work, but a responsible contractor will install drainage culverts where necessary, make use of various types of sediment barriers and waterbars, fill and grade as necessary, and in areas of critical disturbance will even revegetate the terrain with grass seed, fertilizer and mulch. Your forester-advisor can recommend specific companies that have a reputation for being conscientious and "terrain friendly."

In looking more specifically at the trees themselves, all species fall into two categories; they're either softwoods or hardwoods. As a rule, softwoods, which predominantly are the conifer species (pines, spruces, firs, cedars) serve wildlife primarily in terms of cover and, with the exception of white and red cedar, have little food value. Commercial harvesting of pines produces a marginal financial return; these species yield relatively low

Generally, several logging companies bid on timber sales, but accepting the highest bid isn't always in your best interests. Ask your forestry-advisor which companies use the most "terrain friendly" logging practices.

grade timber that generally goes into construction framing lumber or pulpwood for the paper mills.

Hardwoods are where the money is, with the most valuable species being oak, walnut, maple, cherry, ash, hickory, and birch. These species generally go into high-grade construction such as furniture and veneer. Lower-grade hardwoods, which are less valuable, include species such as poplar, beech, sycamore, and elm. These species generally go into the manufacture of construction lumber, flooring, plywood, crates and boxes, pallets and the like.

Ideally, from a wildlife manager's standpoint, the best hardwoods to harvest are those which have trunks that are minimally of 16 inches in diameter and are straight and branch-free to a height of at least 18 feet; these trees command the highest prices commercially and yet are the least beneficial to wildlife. Conversely, hardwoods that have numerous branches, forked trunks and wide-sprawling crowns have far less commercial value,

yet these are the very trees that should be left standing because they produce bountiful seed and mast crops for deer and other forest inhabitants.

With regard to many tree species we can be still more selective. Take oaks, for example. East of the Mississippi there are over 30 different oak species, yet not all are equal in terms of wildlife value. In managing specifically for deer, you'll

The sale of desirable hardwoods such as the oaks generates the most income, while softwoods such as conifers generate the lowest income.

NORTHCOUNTRY WHITETAILS

While hardwood tree species produce income, a wise land manager leaves many of
them standing because of the bountiful nut and seed crops that deer and other
wildlife depend upon.

want to leave most of those in the broad white oak family, especially the
pin-oak and swamp chestnut oak, as their acorns are the most nutritious,
tasty and highly sought out by deer. Conversely, red oaks, black oaks and
most of the others produce acorns which are high in tannic acid and bitter
tasting. Since the acorns of these oaks are not sought out by deer unless
little other food is available, you might as well harvest them, even if
specific trees are producing bountiful acorn crops.

With hickory trees, save the shagbark and shellbark species because
within the broad category of hickories these two yield mast that is highly
favored by squirrels. Unless I'm clearing an area for a specific planting—
say, a deep-wood's food plot to go into clover—I allow all beech trees to
remain. Their commercial value is low-grade, yet the beechnuts they bear
are highly sought by deer, squirrels and especially turkeys. Moreover, beech
trees are typically disfigured and misshapen, with many gnarled branches
and random holes and cavities in their trunks, so they also serve as sought-
after roosting trees by turkeys and prime den sites for squirrels, owls and
countless species of songbirds. Two other tree species I invariably leave
standing are sugar maple and boxelder, as they can be tapped to make syrup.

Incidentally, to assist in one's forestland management, I strongly suggest obtaining at any bookstore a small pocket manual of trees that details where each species grows and has illustrations showing their leaf and bark shapes for easy identification.

As a rule, logging activities on private land are done during the months of November through April because it's easier to work with a stand of timber when leaves are absent, the sap is down and there is no tall ground-vegetation to impede logging crews and their equipment. Also keep in mind that one's land-base is never entirely logged-off all at one time; the five-percent rule is standard and ensures an environmentally sound and economically viable harvest every year, indefinitely.

This ongoing, annual work is of great benefit to deer and other wildlife because it produces a very uneven-aged, diverse ecosystem. Conversely, it's the look-but-don't-touch attitudes of preservationists that constitutes poor forest management because allowing a forest monoculture to exist often permits the outbreak of an otherwise minor insect or disease problem, or even a small lightning-caused fire, to quickly spread and cause extensive, forest-wide damage.

There is yet a final aspect to the periodic logging-off of saleable timber and that's the related sale of firewood. When the sawlogs and veneer trees

**Only a small percentage of trees comprising a land-base are harvested in a given year. The remainder are permitted to continue growing while simultaneously providing food and cover for wildlife.**

are removed from the land, left behind will be countless "slashings." These are unmarketable log sections where a portion of the trunk is forked or knotty, or previously incurred wind damage, or for some other reason is commercially unusable. Plus there will be many large branches littering the ground where each tree was taken down. With a chainsaw, much of this wood can be reduced to firewood at your convenience and reserved for your own use or sold at roadside or through a classified ad in the local newspaper to generate still more income from the land.

The enormous quantity of remaining branches that are too small even for firewood have many uses: Throw them into nearby, deep gullies to help retard the erosion effects occurring there as a result of run-off rainwater; stack them into high piles to serve as hiding cover and nesting habitat for deer, rabbits, squirrels, gamebirds and songbirds; during the dead of winter, when other food is scarce, deer will even flock to such sites to devour the still-tender branchtips and other browse that previously was inaccessible to them but now is at ground-level.

All of this works out very nicely for the landowner because the dead of winter, especially north of the Mason-Dixon Line, is invariably a slow time of year for tending food plots and engaging in other wildlife management projects that must wait until the spring thaw. And, happily, as it usually turns out, his paycheck from the logging company usually arrives just in time to cover the costs of seed and fertilizer for his upcoming spring food plot plantings and other field-work.

We'll have much more to say about trees in forthcoming chapters where we look at the planting of fruit-bearing species that are favored by deer and other wildlife, and especially the conifers when we begin establishing wildlife cover, shelterbelts and windbreaks.

## SHARECROPPING

One of the most viable ways to generate income from open fields and other idle ground, without actually getting involved in the expense and work-intensive activity of farming the land as a livelihood, is engaging in a cooperative crop-production effort with a neighboring farmer. When we purchased our place more than 20 years ago, I initially had no money to invest in wildlife management. So I made the land go to work for me. Since our place is surrounded on all sides by working farms, I began making friends with my new neighbors. One of them expressed an interest in planting corn on one of my 4 acre weed fields, doing it "on the shares."

This is a very common practice in farm country, whereby you allow someone to plant a crop on your land free of charge and, in return, at harvest time, he gives you 25 percent of the crop. Many landowners use their share of the crop to feed their own livestock, if they have any, but usually they sell it back to the farmer that planted it. But I told the farmer, "leave my one-acre share standing in the field, in a square block in the corner bordered by my

One of numerous ways the land can pay for itself is by sharecropping in which a neighbor farmer pays to plant a crop on idle acres.

forestland." I now had in place my very first food plot for deer!

The same year, another neighbor farmer asked to plant soybeans on another 6 acre field. I again did it on the shares and soon had another food plot in place.

As it happened, the very first deer I took on my new place was a doe that was fattening on the soybeans, and that same year my son took a 6-point buck that was coming through the forest to the corn.

But that's not the end of the story. I also had an idle 16-acre field. The neighbor who had planted the corn asked if he could use that acreage to put in a crop of sorghum. Since sorghum isn't high on my list as a food plot for deer, I didn't care for a share of the crop to be left standing, so I countered with an offer to simply rent the 16 acres for that one year, knowing the little waste spillage residue at harvest time would at least attract and benefit turkeys and gamebirds, and he agreed to the deal. My real motive, however, was the $35 per acre rental fee he offered. Remember, this was over 20 years ago and I used that $560 to purchase my first tractor. It was an old clunker, but it ran and I was proud as hell to have it. Moreover, it allowed me the next several years to put in my own food plots.

Working with neighboring landowners, either on the shares or on an annual rental basis, is one of the best ways to get started in wildlife management. The land itself greatly helps to pay its own way, plus the education you receive in being around farmers, continually observing and asking questions, is priceless.

## OTHER INCOME-GENERATING IDEAS

In just looking around your place, and putting on your thinking cap, you're sure to see many ways in which you can harvest money from your acreage that can be used to finance your involvement in food plots and other wildlife projects.

• Do a tree survey and if you have a good number of maples and box elders, contact someone locally who makes syrup and ask if he'd like to tap your trees next winter, either on the shares or for a modest fee.

• Many tracts of acreage see the presence of several old outbuildings—barns, former homesteads with their roofs falling in, sheds and the like—that are in ramshackle condition and should be torn down. In carefully dismantling these structures you'll become the beneficiary of a wealth of wood products that craftsmen, interior decorators and artists are eager to obtain. Just a few examples include: hand-hewn beams that can be used in log cabin construction or cut to length for fireplace mantles; prime oak, walnut and cherry planks that can be used for interior decorating and remodeling; large hand-hewn sandstone blocks and old bricks that can be used in landscaping; roofing slate, knotty and distressed boards, and metal hardware that's in high demand by artists.

• The land you purchase may have one or more hay meadows or fenced pasturelands you'd eventually like to transform into food plots or wildlife cover. But until you're ready to do so, you can immediately begin tapping them for income. Generally, farmers buy existing hay in the field, either on the shares or on a per-bale basis, and they do all the work involved in its mowing, baling and removal. Pastureland is usually rented monthly for feeding livestock on a per-head or cow-calf basis.

# CHAPTER 3

## ANALYZING YOUR
## SOIL & WATER

It has been said that, with many of life's endeavors, most people don't plan to fail. They fail to plan, and this is especially true when it comes to putting in food plots for deer and other wildlife species.

The particular food a land manager has selected may be one that will greatly enhance his wildlife numbers and their health, but keep in mind that it's in seed-form and must first be planted in the soil.

Also keep in mind that

The most successful food plots are those in which the planting is perfectly mated to the medium. But a soil analysis shows this is rarely the case and that lime and a particular fertilizer-blend must be added.

soil isn't simply dirt. It's a complex medium with a unique composition of physical and chemical properties. Moreover, a sample of this medium taken in a specific location may have quite different attributes than another sample taken only 100 yards away.

As a result, a successful food plot planting is one in which the intended forage crop is perfectly mated to the medium. If the medium isn't acceptable in its naturally occurring state, and in a majority of cases it won't be, it usually can be altered through the addition of lime and a specified fertilizer blend. But in some instances even this, perhaps due to a unique soil type, may still not achieve a good union and the better approach is to consider, at least in that particular place, a different forage planting than what initially may have been in mind.

Of course, no one can know any of this in advance without first having a sample of the soil analyzed by a laboratory. One of my friends, "Mark," wishes he would have done this. Mark plowed and disked two acres of ground, planted alfalfa and then broadcast a fertilizer blend recommended by someone at a farm supply store. How anyone could recommend a particular fertilizer blend without first studying a soil test report is beyond me. But in any event Mark predictably grew only a very nice crop of weeds.

If Mark had researched the matter beforehand, he would have learned that alfalfa is a legume that requires a high soil pH and in most cases this requires the addition of lime. A soil test would have also shown exactly what type of fertilizer, and how much, was required for a successful food

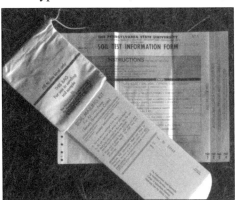

Taking a soil test sample that represents an intended food plot area is quick and easy. Then simply fill out a form telling the lab what you want to plant and mail it in.

plot. Unfortunately, Mark's planting effort, which was doomed from the outset, saw him entirely waste three full days of working time and $280 in expenses.

Getting your soil tested before planting-time is not merely a suggestion. It's a critical necessity. It's also a quick and easy procedure, and it costs next to nothing. Penn State University undoubtedly has the foremost soil lab east of the Mississippi and it's utilized by thousands of farmers and land managers. However, there are countless other labs around the country, as well, and your county extension agent can provide you with a listing of those which most landowners are using in your particular region. The majority of them charge a mere $6 to $10 per soil sample analyzed. All you have to do is call the lab, tell them how many soil-test kits you need, and they'll send them by return mail with a billing invoice enclosed.

## TAKING A SOIL TEST SAMPLE

Acquiring soil samples from the various food plots you intend to plant requires only a few minutes time. And the computer print-out analysis you'll receive from the lab describes in detail exactly what the soil needs in order to successfully grow the particular forage crop you want to establish in that specific location. Also, happily, soil tests do not have to be taken every year. The test results, and the lime and fertilizer recommendations, are nowadays computed for three crop years.

Although a soil test sample can be taken any time of year, I don't advise doing it in the winter or spring. Now, labs are swamped with soil samples by farmers and others who have procrastinated and your test results may be late in arriving; this can cramp your projects if you intend to plant certain foods that should go into the ground as early in the spring as the soil can be worked.

Also, you'll want to allow plenty of time after you receive your test results, and before actual planting, to order lime that may be called for in the test results; once lime is applied, it needs five to six months to break down and be absorbed by the soil so it is in a form that can be utilized by growing plantlife.

Consequently, I prefer to do soil tests sometime in late summer. The ground is not frozen, it's pleasant to work outdoors, the advantage of "time" is on your side, and rainfall usually associated with the upcoming fall months will have had ample opportunity to leach the lime application into the soil by the time you're ready to plant.

First, make a rough sketch of the food plot area you intend to plant. Then on the sketch, depending upon the size of the food plot, make five to ten asterisks (*) that are random but evenly distributed so that when the soil from all the sampling locations is later mixed together you'll have an accurate representation of the entire plot.

As you head afield to actually acquire the soil sample, all you need to take is your sketch, a gallon-size heavy-duty plastic bag with a Zip-Loc closure, and a shovel. At the first asterisk's approximate location, begin by scraping away a 12-inch square area of surface matter (dead leaves, twigs, dry grass and weeds, still-green vegetation, or other debris) to bare soil. Then push your shovel blade down into the ground about six to eight inches deep and remove a one-inch thick slab of soil.

With the edge of the shovel blade, now cut a one inch wide slice of the soil (it should be moist and hold together well). This will give you a one-inch-square by six-inch long "core" that is representative, from top to bottom, of the soil root zone in that specific area.

## PENNSTATE

(814) 863-0841     Fax (814) 863-4540
Agricultural Analytical Services Laboratory
The Pennsylvania State University
University Park PA 16802
http://www.aasl.psu.edu

**SOIL TEST REPORT FOR:**
J WEISS
3589 W GOSHEN RUN
CHESTERHILL OH 43728

**ADDITIONAL COPY TO:**

| DATE | LAB # | SERIAL # | COUNTY | ACRES | ASCS ID | FIELD ID | SOIL |
|------|-------|----------|--------|-------|---------|----------|------|
| 08/23/2001 | S01-04580 | 58033 | Morgan-o | 7 | | Plot 1 | |

**SOIL NUTRIENT LEVELS**

| | | | Below Optimum | Optimum | Above Optimum |
|--|--|--|--|--|--|
| ¹Soil pH | 6.3 | | | | |
| ²Phosphorus (P) | 5 | ppm | | | |
| ²Potassium (K) | 62 | ppm | | | |
| ²Magnesium (Mg) | 162 | ppm | | | |

**RECOMMENDATIONS:** *(See back messages for important information)*

**Limestone\***: 2000 lb/A for a target pH of 6.5.     **Magnesium (Mg):** NONE
*Calcium Carbonate equivalent*

**Plant Nutrients:** *(If manure will be applied, adjust these recommendations accordingly. See back of report.)*

| Year | Crop | Expected Yield | Nitrogen (lb N/A) | Phosphate (lb P₂O₅/A) | Potash (lb K₂O/A) | |
|------|------|----------------|-------------------|----------------------|-------------------|--|
| 1 Planting Ladino Clover | | 2.5 T/A | 0 | 150 | 110 | *See ST2 for other crop recommendations* |
| 2 Planting Ladino Clover | | 2.5 T/A | 0 | 150 | 110 | *See ST2 for other crop recommendations* |
| 3 Planting Ladino Clover | | 2.5 T/A | 0 | 150 | 110 | *See ST2 for other crop recommendations* |

**ADDITIONAL RESULTS:**     **Optional Tests:**

| ¹Calcium (Ca) (ppm) | ²Acidity (meq/100 g) | ³CEC (meq/100 g) | % Saturation of the CEC K | Mg | Ca | Organic Matter % | Nitrate-N ppm | Soluble salts mmhos/cm |
|--|--|--|--|--|--|--|--|--|
| 1863 | 2.0 | 12.8 | 1.2 | 10.5 | 72.6 | | | |

Test Methods: ¹1:1 soil:water pH, ²Mehlich 3 Extractant, ³SMP Buffer pH, ⁴Summation of Cations

4949

**The soil report a land manager receives from a testing lab tells him everything he needs to know about soil additives for a three-year period.**

Next, place the core sample in your plastic bag, fill the hole back in, then move on to the next asterisk location marked on your sketch and repeat the procedure until you've sampled the entire food plot area. Back at your equipment building, lay out several thicknesses of newspaper on a flat surface and pour the contents of the plastic bag onto the paper. Crumble up the dirt lumps with your hands, mix it together, spread it out a bit and allow it to air-dry for two days. Finally, from your dried, blended soil, take about two cups and place it in the special soil bag provided in your soil test kit. Fill out the enclosed form with your general information (name, address, etc.).

Be sure on the form to indicate what was planted in that specific food plot the previous year or what is currently growing there. And of greatest importance of all, be sure to indicate what you want to plant there during the next, upcoming season.

One other thing goes back to the subject of going afield to obtain the soil in the first place. If you plan to take soil test samples for several different food plots in different locations, be sure to use a felt-tipped pen with indelible ink to label the outside of each plastic collection bag. This way, there's no chance your accumulation of many bags will become mixed up; otherwise, it's easy to become confused and forget which bag of sampled soil was taken where.

Lastly, place the soil bag and your completed information form in the larger bag provided with the kit and mail it to the lab of your choice. Within two weeks you'll receive a computer printout telling you everything you need to know about the soil and, of greatest importance, what type and amount of fertilizer and lime you need to add to the soil to ensure a robust crop of the type you intend to plant.

## WATER TESTING

As a rule, in most regions of the country, so-called "sheet water" and "static water" are sufficient to provide for the needs of deer and other wildlife. Sheet water is slowly moving surface water, most often in the form of rivers, streams, creeks, run-off trickles from higher ground, and spring seepages. Or it is static in form where a combination of sheet water and rainwater is permitted to accumulate in ponds, lakes, reservoirs, and stock tanks. However, in extremely arid regions, or in regions where sheet water or static water are only seasonal, landowners commonly "develop" more reliable and consistent water sources.

A pond on the property is a valuable asset to ensuring the year-around presence of water for many wildlife species. It also provides the landowner with other forms of recreation.

One example might be a dry stream bed, where a backhoe operator can be hired for a few hours to dig out intermittent holes every several hundred yards that will fill and serve as collection pools when the stream is running and then continue to serve as holding pools when the stream is dry.

**If a property has small streams that typically dry-up in summer, find intermittent damp spots and then hire a backhoe operator to dig out depressions that will serve as seepage collection basins.**

Or, a pond may be built to service multiple uses, with water for wildlife being just one consideration and side benefits being the creation of an attractive location for ducks and geese, fishing opportunities, and even irrigation of nearby food plots during periods of drought.

It's also common for landowners to develop springs. The procedure is to first find a sloping hillside area where surface water seepage is evident; you probably already know of certain places on your land that are perpetually wet and may even have cattails and marsh grass growing there.

A backhoe operator is then hired to dig out a trench through the spring area; the average dimensions are six feet deep by two feet wide by 40 feet in length. In the trench is laid a length of perforated plastic pipe with a T-fitting in the middle. The trench is then filled with several feet of gravel and then the original fill-dirt. From the T-fitting, an solid-wall extension pipe runs underground, downhill, to some type of collection container such as a sheet metal or formed-concrete tank that holds several hundred gallons. From that point on, the spring continuously gravity-feeds the collection tank year-around, with an outlet run-off pipe allowing excess water to escape from the tank.

A drilled well also is a possibility, but this usually is the most expensive option because an installed pumping system is required along with electricity (or a windmill) to serve it.

In any of these efforts, first consult with your county extension agent. Based upon the predominant water sources and soil types in your region, he can recommend the most economical and popular water-

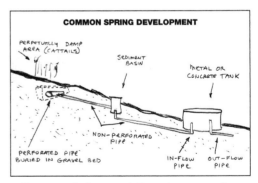

**If a property has no static water, or running water such as a stream, developing a spring is the most economical alternative. In farming regions, many contractors specialize in this type of work.**

collection procedures used in your particular county, as well as local contractors that frequently engage in that type of work.

With plentiful water now made available, it's wise to next have the water's chemistry evaluated by a local lab that specializes in water analysis. After all, you don't want to poison the wildlife you're managing or any other critters that come to drink!

Actually, this rarely happens, but precautions nevertheless are advised. The primary culprits are nearly always in one of three forms: Unusually high levels of lead or arsenic naturally present in the soil in that specific region; exceedingly high levels of coliform bacteria as a result of former livestock operations on nearby higher ground, such as pastureland, corrals, feedlots or barns where manure has accumulated over the course of many years (or decades); or, where former agricultural croplands were planted for many years and, in time, residual pesticide and herbicide run-off has contaminated the ground water in that specific location.

Having your water analyzed is no more complicated than requesting a water-sample kit from a local lab. It will contain a capped, sterile tube or jar, and an instruction sheet. Within two weeks you'll receive a printout detailing the water's chemistry and what corrective measures, if any, are necessary to make it fit for animal (or human) consumption.

As with soil tests, separate water samples are required for different regions of the property; the average cost for a water sample analysis is $20.

**Tip:** Static (non-moving) water sources commonly develop an algae problem which, if left unchecked, will eventually cause deer and other wildlife to refuse to drink the water. In the case of small-capacity metal or concrete holding tanks where developed-spring run-off water collects, the popular remedy is to simply take an 18-inch length of copper wire, coil it, and place it in the tank. The minuscule amount of

Static (non-moving) water sources such as ponds and springs should periodically have their chemistry tested by a lab to ensure it's safe; in a majority of cases it is, but if certain hard metals are present, neutralizing agents can be added.

copper that leaches from the wire into the water will kill algae but is entirely harmless to deer, other wildlife species, pets, and humans.

In the case of larger water-containment systems, such as ponds, the standard remedy is adding copper sulfate to the water. CSu is available in crystal form at all farm-supply stores and it is broadcast-spread across the surface of the water by randomly throwing handfuls. It, too, will kill algae and in recommended application rates is harmless to fish, wildlife, pets, and humans. Consult your local department of fish and wildlife for recommended application procedures in accordance with the calculated acre-feet of water contained within the pond basin.

---

## SOIL TESTING AGENCIES

**Agricultural Analytical
Services Lab**
Penn State University
University Park, PA 16802
(814) 863-0841
www.aasl.psu.edu

**Antler King**
W11353 Spaulding Rd.
Black River Falls, WI 54615
(715) 284-9547
www.antlerking.com

**Whitetail Institute
of North America**
Route 1, Box 3006
Pintlala, AL 36043
(800) 688-3030
www.deernutrition.com

---

## WATER TESTING AGENCIES

Since water samples must be analyzed in their fresh state, and must not have been subjected to temperature extremes, using a mail service to a distant lab destination is not recommended.

Good advice is to call your county extension agent and ask for the name of the water analysis lab most other landowners in your immediate area are using. Most states have numerous labs, so simply call the closest one and ask for a test kit to be mailed to you. Upon receiving the test kit, read the instructions, take the water sample, fill out the enclosed form, then hand deliver the sample to the lab.

# CHAPTER 4

## LIME & FERTILIZER
# APPLICATIONS

One of the most important aspects of a soil analysis is determining the soil's pH level. pH is a measure of the soil's present level of acidity or alkalinity. On a soil pH scale of 0 to 14, a pH of 7.0 is considered neutral. As the pH rises above 7.0 it becomes more alkaline (or "basic"). As the pH

falls below 7.0 it becomes more acidic. Moreover, just one unit of change represents a tenfold change in acidity or alkalinity. For example, if a pH of 7.0 drops to a pH of 6.0, many land managers might not consider this to be a dramatic change, but it is; it represents a change in the soil chemistry that has become ten times more acidic!

Plants consume nutrients from the soil, as do deer and other wildlife species that consume those plants. If the plants are to continue to thrive, and, so too, the wildlife, the land manager must regularly replenish lost soil nutrients.

## HOW DOES SOIL ACIDITY OCCUR AND WHY IS IT THE BANE OF SUCCESSFUL FOOD PLOTS?

It occurs for many reasons, one of the most common being the simple age-old decomposition of leaves and twigs falling onto food plots from adjacent forested areas but likewise because of the normal transition into fall-winter dormancy of food plot plants themselves. Also, when deer and various other wildlife species consume food plot plantlife, they in turn consume the alkalinity properties the plants have absorbed from the soil, thereby slowly but steadily depleting the soil and thus lowering its pH.

Whatever the reason for reduced soil alkalinity, it sharply reduces the activity of soil microbes and successful insect pollination of many plant species. Even more important, the pH level of the soil determines how well your plants will be able to use the nutrients in the soil, and different plant species have different abilities to accomplish this process.

As a rule, a neutral pH of 7.0, or one that's 6.5 (just slightly acidic) is best for the majority of plant species. Soils that are highly acid (lower than 6.0) typically have high concentrations of aluminum, iron, and manganese, which can inhibit plant growth. In still other instances, a low pH soil can even be toxic to certain plant species.

**Lime is particularly important to clover blends, alfalfa and all other legumes such as peas and beans.**

Happily, when lime is added to the soil, the pH level rises and, in so doing, toxic substances are neutralized. Moreover, the plants now can efficiently utilize the nutrients in the soil, primarily those which you've applied in the form of fertilizer.

Yet bear in mind that liming is not a permanent cure and additional lime applications will have to occasionally be made in years to come, in accordance with the results of future soil test samples; as a rule, clay soils generally hold lime longer than sandy soils but require more lime to raise the pH to a specified level than would be required in a sandy soil.

A change in the type of plant species one desires to put into a particular food plot area may also require a lime-application change; for example, legumes (all beans, all peas, all clovers, alfalfa and lespedeza) require a higher pH (and more lime) than most other vegetative species. So if you have a soil test sample taken, in order to put a food plot into corn, but the following year decide to not put corn into that same plot again but instead to plant clover or alfalfa, you'll need another soil test because those latter two species are members of the legume family and thus require a higher pH.

## HOW MUCH LIME?

It usually takes a significant quantity of lime to even moderately change a soil's pH. So if a soil-test analysis of an intended food plot calls for a lime application, it invariably will be described in your report in terms of required tons-per-acre. The soil-test results also will describe the type of lime that should be applied for your specified crop-planting intentions. Lime is available in the form of pulverized limestone rock, pellets, granules, or finely ground powder; naturally, the finer textures are absorbed into the soil more quickly than the coarser sizes, yet conversely they do not last as long and must be replenished more frequently.

For small food plots, no larger than one-half acre, lime can be purchased in granular or powder form at any farm supply store. It's generally put up in 50-pound bags and can then be applied with a commercial spreader of the type otherwise used to broadcast seed or fertilizer by being pulled behind a tractor or mounted on the rear chassis of an ATV or even a pick-up truck.

However, for food plots larger than one-half acre, buying lime in bag form and applying it yourself is prohibitively expensive; bags of pelleted lime cost as much as ten-times more than bulk quantities of equivalent agricultural lime.

Applying bagged lime also is very time-consuming, and often does not result in a uniform distribution across the ground-area to be planted. With some simple math it's easy to see how labor-intensive this can be. If you have an intended two-acre food plot that requires two tons of lime per acre, that's a total of four tons (8,000 pounds) of required lime. In turn, that means you'll need to purchase (and transport to the planting site, and spread) 80 of those 50-pound bags, just for that one food plot!

Clearly, this won't do. Instead, the best advice is to check the "agricultural and farm supplies" section of your phone

Lime generally is applied at a rate of tons-per-acre, so most land managers hire a lime distributor to apply it. Then the lime should be lightly disked into the ground because it takes the soil several months to absorb it and make it available to plantlife.

NORTHCOUNTRY WHITETAILS

book's yellow pages for a dealer that sells and applies lime in economical bulk form. Or simply ask a neighbor farmer for the name of the local lime distributor he and his friends regularly use.

The standard procedure in ordering lime is to tell the dealer how many acres you need to have limed, how many tons per acre should be applied, and in what form. The dealer will then arrive at your intended planting site in a large vehicle somewhat resembling a dump truck but with wide flotation tires to easily drive over the food plots without leaving ruts. After calibrating the truck's spreader mechanism to your lime requirements per acre, he'll then make several passes across the ground to evenly distribute the mineral; the spreader will throw it out and to the sides of the truck in approximate 25-yard-wide swaths. In most instances, an average two-acre food plot can be completely limed to your soil-test specifications in about 20 minutes.

Finally, it should be noted that a lime application begins working the most quickly if it's soon thereafter rained upon and thus washed into the soil. Since a lime application laying on the top of very dry soil has virtually no effect, if there is no rain in the immediate forecast you can at least help the effort along by lightly disking the ground; in this manner, as soon as rain does come, the lime will far more quickly be absorbed deep into the soil than otherwise.

## A LOOK AT BENEFICIAL FERTILIZERS

As with humans, plantlife needs nutrition. It's as simple as that, and as complicated. Whenever someone managing land for wildlife experiences problems, it's usually somehow related to plant nutrition and the beginning of a domino effect.

In other words, if a given food plot is suffering a nutrition deficit, perhaps by overbrowsing by too many animals utilizing that particular food source, things can quickly get out of hand. First, the plantlife does not experience a rapid growth-recovery in order to regenerate itself. This makes it susceptible to stress, particularly during weather extremes, which in turn may weaken the food plot's natural immunity and make it vulnerable to disease or insect damage.

At the beginning of this book I expressed the opinion, based upon many years of involvement with wildlife and agriculture, that Mother Nature is a bitch. You're constantly fighting her, and an accepted tenet of farming is that occasionally you'll lose a battle. So the best that one can do is diligently strive to minimize one's losses and then, simply put, cross your fingers.

Attending to a food plot's nutritional needs is just one of many ways of attempting to stack the deck in your favor. As we've previously seen, liming the ground is essential. But also, when plants remove nutrients from the soil, and then deer and other critters next begin removing the plant's created biomass, those soil nutrients must be replaced if the next generation of plantlife is to thrive. It's an ongoing cycle, and it's accomplished through the regular applications of commercial fertilizer. Three key players in this plantlife process are nitrogen, phosphorus and potassium, commonly referred to in the ag business as NPK.

To provide a dramatic example of how quickly soil can become depleted of essential nutrients, consider a one-acre deer food plot planted to ever-popular alfalfa. To put this in a visual perspective, one acre of ground, in terms of square footage, is equivalent in size to a professional football field. And during the course of just one year, that alfalfa crop will remove from the soil 480 pounds of potassium. Since alfalfa has a healthy appetite, it also will remove from the same one acre an estimated 120 pounds of phosphorus and 450 pounds of nitrogen. Clearly, then, if alfalfa is planted but not "fed" the above nutrients on an annual basis, it will soon dwindle and revert to an infertile weedfield until mankind once again intervenes.

Although a soil-test sample to measure soil fertility is good for three years, a food plot planted to a legume should have it's pH tested every year. Inexpensive, do-it-yourself kits are available to the land manager.

Fertilizer is a blended ratio of nitrogen, phosphorus and potassium, known as NPK. Using his soil-test sample results, a land manager can fertilize food plots himself using a mechanical spreader attached to an ATV or tractor.

Of course, it's beyond the scope of this book to intensively look at commercial fertilizers, much less examine in detail the nutritive needs of myriad species of plantlife commonly put into deer food plots; entire agronomy textbooks have been devoted to individual plant species such as alfalfa, corn, wheat, oats, soybeans and others, and just as many other available books focus even more narrowly upon the chemistry of individual fertilizer components.

But by presenting an overview of fertilizers, the sportsman will have a better grasp of how to "feed" his foodplots and in turn make them attractive to deer and other targeted wildlife species.

## BENEFITS OF POTASSIUM

In the plant world, potassium, in cooperation with other elements, takes on a wide variety of assignments. It's critical in photosynthesis, moisture retention during droughts, and subsequently the production of protein. The protein, in turn, is essential to deer in regulating their bodily fluids, nerve and muscle function, and creating antler growth.

Potassium also enhances the disease-resistance of plantlife and instills it with vigor, and this brings up an important aspect of putting in food plots for deer and other wildlife. One activity a land manager involves himself with on a weekly basis is simply walking around to look at his food plots, but his goal is not merely to admire his work. He's looking for evidence of mildew on plant leaves, leaf margins that are beginning to appear scorched, weak stalks, small seed pods, undeveloped root mass and short tap roots. Any of these usually signal a potassium deficiency. In ground terrain, the greatest quantities of naturally occurring potassium are not found in the soil itself but in rocks and therefore the mineral is only minimally available to

High levels of potassium and phosphorus in the plants that deer eat afford many health benefits but they especially contribute to large antler growth.

plantlife during the very slow process of "weathering." In pioneer times, our ancestors solved this problem by applying to the ground ashes from burned trees; that's why, today, potassium is still sometimes referred to as "potash."

In these modern times, however, the land manager who must apply potassium to the soil does so by adding phosphate rock which has been crushed into granular form and is part of an overall fertilizer blend containing other ingredients. How much potassium to apply, and when, is easily determined. Read your soil-test report!

## BENEFITS OF PHOSPHORUS

Phosphorus is likewise a vital nutrient on behalf of both plant and animal life. In a mature deer, the vast majority of its body-phosphorus is found within its bone structure, and this means that in bucks it's critical to antler development and mass. The body metabolisms of deer and other wildlife species are also highly dependent upon phosphorus because it regulates the proper utilization of fats, carbohydrates and amino acids, and aids in the development of muscle tone.

Plantlife also is highly dependent upon an adequate phosphorus level, especially in the development of a healthy root structure that can facilitate the uptake of water and other nutrients from the soil to foster the rapid growth of stems, leaves and eventually flower buds, seed pods, fruits or berries. Since all of these plant-parts are in turn heavily utilized by deer, soil-phosphorus levels become steadily depleted with each day of the growing season.

In doing his regular walk-arounds to inspect his food plots, the land manager will want to be on the lookout for several telltale indications of a phosphorus deficiency. The two most common signs are stunted growth and plant leaves that are beginning to reveal a reddish wine color.

Even soil that is otherwise very fertile may be phosphorus-deficient because, like potassium, much of it is contained in rock and released only very slowly during weathering. However, unlike potassium, trace amounts of phosphorus which are indeed released by rock quickly bond with other minerals (aluminum and iron, in particular) and, in so doing, become "locked up" and unavailable to plantlife and in turn are unavailable to animals that eat those plants.

As with naturally-occurring soil phosphorus, phosphorus added by the land manager will likewise eventually begin to lock up, which means that he must make phosphorus applications on a regular basis so that his plantlife has the mineral available on a steady and recurring basis. In many cases the most efficient way to accomplish this is by using a fertilizer of the slow-release variety that ensures a continual, adequate phosphorus level through the duration of the growing season. How much phosphorus to apply, and when, is easily determined. Read your soil-test report!

## BENEFITS OF NITROGEN

Nitrogen completes the soil-mineral triad and it's essential to a plant's ability to engage in photosynthesis and the production of amino acids which in turn govern the production of protein; the chain of command then sees the protein compounds passed along to deer and other wildlife species that consume the plantlife.

In doing his periodic walk-arounds, the land manager will want to be especially alert to plant leaves that formerly in the growing season were a healthy-looking dark green in color but now are slowly beginning to turn yellow; a sure sign of nitrogen-depletion in the soil. But a nitrogen-deficiency may manifest itself in other ways as well, as in the case of plants that remain green in color but are unusually slow-growing or even becoming stunted; in this context, "stunted" means the plants appear mature in shape (conformation) but are abnormally small in size.

Naturally occurring soil-nitrogen is a by-product of the decomposition of plant and animal life. But this process is so slow that it is not readily available to new plant life. However, many plant species—the legumes in particular, such as alfalfa, various clovers, and soybeans—have the ability to at least slightly compensate for a shortage of soil-nitrogen by extracting it from the atmosphere and "fixing" it on root nodules so it is available to the plant. Yet this is never quite enough, thus requiring the land manager to periodically add it to the soil.

Unlike potassium and phosphorus, nitrogen is considered a highly "movable" nutrient, meaning that it can migrate in accordance with soil-type and moisture.

Hence, in sandy or sloping soil in particular, too much rainfall can literally percolate a nitrogen application away, leaching it so deep into the soil, or far from its application area, that it's largely unavailable or exclusively unavailable to the targeted plantlife.

As a result, it's a common practice to provide some types of food plots with at least one renewed application of nitrogen during each growing season; in the case of sprawling ground-cover crops such as clover, the procedure is known as "top-dressing," while in the case of row crops such as corn it's known as "side dressing." How much nitrogen to apply, and when, is easily determined. Read your soil-test report!

## NPK FORMULATIONS

One detriment resulting from the addition of nitrogen to the soil is that it increases the soil's acidity (lowers the pH). This brings us full-circle back to the beginning of this chapter where we discussed the importance of periodically adding lime to food plots to raise the pH, particularly where legumes (that need alkaline soil) are to be planted or presently are being grown.

So-called "fertilizer" is basically a blend of nitrogen (N), phosphorus (P) and potassium (K) in certain ratios in accordance with specific application needs. In some cases other ingredients are added to the blend, such as pelleted lime for example.

An NPK blend, therefore, is stated in terms of a numerical name such as 12-12-12 (also called "triple-twelve") or 6-12-24 or whatever, with the first number of the triad always representing the percentage of nitrogen, the second being the percentage of phosphorus and the third being potassium. It's not necessary for a land manager to compute the ratio of mathematical percentages; simply take your soil test report to the farm-supply outlet where the fertilizer is to be purchased and they'll provide the correct blend.

When actually applying the fertilizer to your intended food plots, it is,

NORTHCOUNTRY WHITETAILS

Anytime a food plot appears thin, stunted, or spotty, the land manager should first suspect a low or imbalanced fertilizer that has caused plant-nutrient stress.

however, your responsibility to correctly calculate the spreading rate, which is usually a factor of volume and vehicle speed. This is easily accomplished by consulting the operator's guide sheet that came with the spreader equipment and properly calibrating it; for example, with the spreader I'm currently using, I know that applying 100 pounds of blended fertilizer per acre is easily accomplished by simply setting the spreader dial at the 100 mark, filling the hopper with 100 pounds of the fertilizer, then driving at approximately 3 miles-per-hour and making repeated passes back and forth to evenly distribute the fertilizer until the hopper is empty.

In addition to NPK, generic fertilizer may also contain smaller amounts of other ingredients such as magnesium, calcium and sulphur. And a specialty fertilizer, such as that intended for alfalfa, may contain boron, which is needed in a higher amount than other perennial grasses.

Some companies that sell seeds commonly planted in food plots also sell specialty food plot fertilizers. They're not significantly different than the blends sold at your farm-supply outlet, they're far more expensive than if purchased locally, and the shipping costs will kill you.

In future chapters we'll have more to say about lime and fertilizer applications when we more specifically look at common food plot plantings.

# CHAPTER 5

## EQUIPMENT NEEDED TO
# PLANT FOOD PLOTS

It stands to reason that the intended sizes and locations of food plots often guide the land manager's equipment choices needed to work those pieces of land. So let's first look at that subject.

Of course, our primary intention with food plots is to feed deer and other wildlife. But we should strive to have more forage growing in our plots than what the local wildlife population can readily consume. This approach will permit our planting to last a long time (as in the case of annual cereal grains and legumes such as peas and beans) or to easily and quickly regenerate itself (as in the case of perennial legumes such as clovers).

Therefore, as a general rule, the smallest food plots should never be less than one-half acre in size, simply because even a modest number of deer can over-browse such a small feeding area; keep in mind that other critters such as turkeys, ducks and geese, and small game may periodically show up to likewise eat their fill. Also, as a rule, the largest food plots should be

Food-plot size is a balancing act. They should be large enough that deer can not quickly deplete them, but if they're too large they can become very expensive and time-consuming to plant and maintain.

restricted to no more than three or four acres in size. Otherwise, the expense of planting and maintaining them can become prohibitive, and the intensive labor involved will have you sometimes thinking you've gotten yourself involved in full-time farming.

As long as we've described ideal food plots as ranging in size from one to four acres, we should also say a few words about the types of ideal locations where a land manager should plant them. Of course, as we'll see later, various plantlife species often have preferred types of soil, drainage characteristics and the like, but for the moment let's look in terms of broader considerations. Food plots situated in deep-wood's regions are of great benefit to wildlife because deer and other critters feel at ease visiting them even during midday. However, you'll want to ensure that each specific deep-wood's area under consideration is not in full-shade throughout the day or your plantings won't do well; in many cases you can slightly open-up the surrounding tree canopy to allow longer daily periods of sunlight to bathe the ground.

Of great importance, keep in mind that other food plots situated in more open areas should be concentrated near the interior portions of the land you own or have control over. Otherwise, if any of the plots are near the outer perimeters, you'll experience "neighborly drift" in which those who own property bordering your's but don't plant food and cover to enhance wildlife populations will continually attempt to capitalize upon your investments and hard work.

Similarly, if the property you own or control is relatively large in size, and is bisected by one or more county or township roads, strive to avoid putting

Food-plot location is important. Ideally, they should be located away from human disturbance and adjacent to thick cover so deer and other wildlife feel comfortable utilizing them even during midday.

your food plots in locations where animals must regularly cross the roads to gain access to the prime feeding areas; this situation, and their return travels to their security cover, exposes them to deadly encounters with vehicles, poachers and road hunters.

As we'll see in coming chapters, the food plots that are the most attractive to wildlife are those bordered on at least three sides by dense security cover. Deer in particular like to be able to approach a feeding area without exposing themselves, begin feeding, and then upon the slightest whim return to that thick cover with one or two quick jumps.

## EQUIPMENT CHOICES

Obviously, various equipment choices must be tailored to the average food plot sizes being planted on a given property. If the plots are relatively small, the equipment will likewise have to be down-sized so that it's capable of a tight turning radius and can be maneuvered in close quarters. This is especially the case with those small food plots bordered on two or more sides by extremely steep terrain, dense cover, a natural terrain feature such as a stream, and those plots situated in deep-wood's regions.

A great benefit of down-sized equipment is its moderate purchase price and its economical maintenance and fuel costs.

Conversely, the largest food plots require somewhat larger and more efficient equipment choices. Otherwise, you'll pay in terms of sweat equity. The downside is that larger equipment is more costly to purchase, and main-

With the largest food plots, preferably no more than 4 acres, a mid-size tractor and assorted pull-behind implements is cost-effective in terms of time saved. A front-end loader is a highly desirable option. Establish a good working relationship with a local dealer, because parts and supplies are needed for routine maintenance.

tenance and fuel expenses will be significantly higher.

If the land manager is not mechanically inclined to do much more than minor equipment maintenance such as routine engine-oil and hydraulic-oil changes, lube jobs, replacing belts and hoses, and the like, I strongly suggest purchasing major equipment items from a local, reputable farm-equipment dealer.

It's risky business, and can be financially devastating, to buy equipment sold as-is from a private owner or, worse yet, at a farm auction; unless, that is, you have the tools and knowledge to tackle major repairs and really enjoy tearing down and rebuilding engines and transmissions.

Conversely, when you purchase from a local dealer various equipment items that are either new, or used but in excellent condition, you also buy peace of mind. First, the equipment nearly always is thoroughly "checked out" before being put on the lot for sale, to make sure everything is in good working order. Moreover, if at any time in the near future you need advice regarding the use of the equipment, general maintenance supplies, or even repair service, the dealer you've established a relationship with is only a phone call away.

All of this is extremely important because in the planting of food plots, just as in large-scale farming operations, "timing" is a critical element. There usually are only very narrow windows of opportunity in which the weather, available soil moisture, and soil temperature are ideal for the completion of tasks. Plus, you have to coordinate all of this with the ordering of seed and fertilizer, scheduling the delivery and spreading of lime, and ground preparation, not to mention myriad job and family responsibilities.

So naturally, if a particular equipment item critical to the completion of a given task unexpectedly goes on the fritz, you need help, and you need it right now! And farm dealers commonly give preferential treatment to those regular customers who have previously bought equipment and supplies from them. I've actually had mechanics come to my farm late in the evening and do repair work in the field, by flashlight. Sure, I had to pay overtime but I was able to resume planting at the crack of dawn.

## TRACTORS

When putting in larger-size food plots, a tractor is worth its price in speedy, efficient work. But you don't need one of the gargantuan 500 horse-power models that your neighbor mortgaged his farm to buy in order to plow hundreds of acres of ground.

A mid-size tractor of 30 to 50 horsepower is ideal for a majority of larger-size food plot planting projects. Stay away from the three-wheel, tricycle-type of tractor if you have moderately sloping or steep terrain because they can be "tippy." Go with a conventional four-wheel tractor and, if much of the terrain is not level, have your dealer adjust the spread-width of both the front and rear wheels and "load" the tires with inexpensive, heavy calcium chloride; this will lower the machine's center of gravity and give you maximum, safe stability.

Nowadays, a majority of landowners favor diesel over gasoline engines for the simple reason that diesels are more reliable and maintenance free, and they're more economical to operate. Moreover, you'll need on your tractor a three-point hitch, power-take-off (PTO), drawbar, and hydraulic-line spools, for attaching and using accessory pull-behind equipment items;

nowadays, most tractors have these factory-installed.

When shopping for a tractor, it's worth the additional investment to get one that has an accessory or after-market front-end loader. You'll constantly find yourself using this hydraulic "bucket" for moving piles of dirt and gravel, removing heavy rocks from areas to be planted, transporting bags of seed and fertilizer to planting sites, and much more.

A hydraulic back-blade that quickly attaches to the tractor's rear-mounted three-point hitch is equally handy for grading access roads and trails, filling holes and ruts, and much more.

A tank-type sprayer is needed; most are mounted on a chassis with wheels and pulled behind the tractor, but some types mount on a frame attached to the rear of the tractor. A sprayer handles the chore of applying herbicide to the ground to kill weed growth before planting and to periodically apply insecticide to some plant species. Some land managers prefer to avoid these chemical applications and allow nature to take its course; it's a personal choice and, in making it, the land manager must be willing to sometimes sacrifice as much as 50-percent of a food plot's potential yield to weeds and insects.

For major ground-breaking operations, especially where no crop has previously been planted, you'll need a deep plow; for a majority of food plot plantings, an 18-inch "two-bottom" plow is adequate. For shallow plantings, where ground previously has been broken or where grasses or cereal grains are to be planted, a so-called chisel plow usually is sufficient.

A disk and/or harrow attachment is required for breaking up the large furrows and soil clods turned up by a plow and smoothing the surface of the ground for planting.

A spreader is needed to evenly distribute lime and fertilizer. Two types are available: One is a pull-behind, drop- or trough-type spreader mounted on wheels and which is fully adjustable for the volume and type of material to be distributed; the other is a canister or so-called "cyclone" spreader that resembles a steel drum and is mounted on the rear of the tractor and has a spin-plate that revolves at high speeds and throws the materi-

An after-market tank sprayer that mounts on the back of an ATV serves many needs. This model costs less than $200 and runs off the ATV's 12-volt battery.

al to be distributed.

One or more seed planters are necessary for row crops such as corn or full-coverage crops such as grasses and small grains. For grass plantings, and some small grains, a cultipacker is commonly used to smooth and firm the ground during shallow seed-planting.

A bush-hog used for clearing brush and mowing grass food plots is important to the land manager. This model is pulled behind an ATV; much larger models are made for tractors.

Many land managers nowadays also engage in no-till planting in which the ground is not plowed or disked. A no-till planter is a pull-behind device that opens up a narrow slice in the ground, inserts the seeds and then closes the slice, typically right over the top of the previous year's crop residue. However, no-till equipment is quite expensive; consequently, conservation agencies that promote no-till planting, primarily to prevent erosion, commonly purchase the equipment and then rent it on a daily basis to local landowners. Talk with your county extension agent for details.

Finally, a pull-behind PTO-powered mower (or so-called "bush-hog") is essential to maintenance of grass and legume food plots, clearing areas of brush and high weed growth, maintaining access trails and such.

With regard to any of these equipment items, the many styles available and how to operate and maintain them is beyond the scope of this book.

Heavy-duty equipment items intended primarily for large lawns and gardens are also well-adapted to planting and maintaining smaller food plots only an acre or two in size.

Good advice is to consult with your local farm equipment dealer as to your specific food plot intentions, heed his recommendations, and then follow the owner-operator instruction manual that comes with each equipment item.

Moreover, whenever possible, it's a wise practice to engage in so-called equipment-standardization. Most tractor manufacturers also make implements that are specifically designed to be mated with their tractors. So no matter whether you might prefer a tractor made by John Deere, Ford, New

Holland, Massey-Ferguson, International or whatever, it's usually a good practice to try to acquire accessories that are made by the same companies.

## DOWNSIZED EQUIPMENT

Nowadays, a great many landowners and sportsmen own all-terrain vehicles, also known as ATVs or so-called four-wheelers. If you don't already own one, they're relatively

Increasingly, land managers are using ATVs to put in food plots because they're well-suited to small plots of land and have a tight-turning radius for working irregularly shaped ground-areas.

inexpensive to buy and maintain, easy to learn how to operate, and have a multitude of outdoor uses.

Moreover, the popularity of ATVs has in recent years spawned an explosion in the manufacture of aftermarket, ATV-compatible farm implements that can be used to plow, disk, plant, fertilize and otherwise maintain food plots. These are not toys but the very same types of rugged equipment items designed for use with conventional tractors but simply reduced in size and weight for working small pieces of ground.

As mentioned earlier, the best food plots generally range in size from one to four acres and frequently are situated in woodland areas or other relatively remote regions of the property and tend to be irregular-shaped. And in these frequently confined areas it's far easier and faster to maneuver

Many after-market companies now make available to ATV owners a wide variety of compatible, downsized, ground-working implements for use in establishing and maintaining food plots.

a four-wheeler pulling a compact accessory implement which has a tight-turning radius.

In going back to ATVs themselves, one thing I strongly suggest, if you don't already own one, is to purchase a model with a higher horsepower and four-wheel-drive capability. Some aftermarket, pull-behind equipment items can be quite heavy and "ground-resistant" and you'll greatly appreciate the increased horsepower and traction.

In carrying downsizing to the

extreme, many land managers also make periodic use of still other equipment items that are otherwise intended for large vegetable gardens, estates and golf courses. These include walk-behind machines such as roto-tillers, and heavy-duty mowers for not only grass but clearing tall weeds, brush, and saplings up to two inches thick; with some of these mowers a sulky can even be attached to allow the operator to ride. If the land manager has terrain areas that are unusually steep or rugged, and additionally are small and irregular-shaped, and he already owns such equipment for around-home use, they can play a role in food plot management as well.

## PLOTMASTER: THE ULTIMATE IN EQUIPMENT VERSATILITY

Blaine Burley of Wrightsville, Georgia holds a bachelor's degree in civil engineering, and a master's degree in environmental and natural resource management, both of which have seen him charged with the responsibility of managing thousands of acres of wildlife habitat. So naturally, he's used virtually every type of food plot equipment imaginable, and never was truly satisfied. So he designed his own, dubbed it The Plotmaster, and it has been a raving success with sportsmen/landowners nationwide.

The Plotmaster is pulled behind an ATV, but unlike other aftermarket equipment items it is the pinnacle of versatility. Rather than having to separately purchase individual pieces of accessory equipment, and intermittently have to attach them to perform various field chores, the Plotmaster is a single unit that does it all.

The basic unit comes with an electric or manual lift system, plow attachments, adjustable disk/harrow, cultivator, electric seeder, cultipacker, drag, and carriage unit. Depending upon a land manager's individual needs,

additional accessories can be purchased and attached to the Plotmaster; these include a compactor, aerator, rake, scrape blade, rolling basket, fertilizer spreader, and sprayer. At only four-feet in width, the Plotmaster is ideal for putting in conventional one- to four-acre food plots in the usual places a land manager might choose. But it's also perfect for planting forage

Among ATV owners, the most popular equipment is the Plotmaster, an all-in-one collection of implements so the land manager does not have to switch among equipment items to perform various chores.

items in rough, difficult terrain such as firebreaks, narrow powerline corridors, small openings in deep forest regions, cut-overs, and even the fringes of swampy terrain.

With a Plotmaster, a land manager can plow, disk, and plant a food plot by making only a single pass over the ground area!

Moreover, with the Plotmaster, food plots can be planted with a single pass using a single piece of equipment rather than having to make multiple passes using multiple pieces of equipment. This means that, incredibly, you can plow, disk, seed, cover and cultipack all in one sweep, and with an accessory spreader you can also fertilize at the same time.

It goes without saying but using a Plotmaster saves an enormous amount of time afield, not to mention sharply reduced fuel costs. But the greatest financial savings lie in the fact that the all-in-one Plotmaster is far less expensive than separately purchasing numerous equipment accessories that each are capable of performing only one chore.

## EQUIPMENT SECURITY PRECAUTIONS

Acquiring equipment items for planting and maintaining food plots can amount to a tidy sum. So it's wise to protect your investment from vandalism, thievery, and the weather.

First, never leave valuable equipment in the field at the end of the working day, unless it's in a highly secure area and the weather is forecast to be clear; then, remove the tractor's or ATV's ignition key.

If you're an absentee landowner, it's imperative to have some type of equipment storage building that can be locked. Besides, you'll want a heated, weatherproof structure where you can perform routine equipment maintenance during the off-season. Such a building also allows for the storage of bags of seed and fertilizer, spare equipment parts and supplies, and the wide variety of hand tools landowners invariably need.

Since your investment in all of this may be significant, having it covered by insurance is wise. Consult with your agent and you may find you can purchase a relatively inexpensive rider to your homeowner's policy.

Following is a reference list of companies that specialize in equipment items specifically designed for planting and maintaining food plots.

# FOOD PLOT EQUIPMENT

**Cycle Country**
2188 Hwy 86
Milford, IA 51351
(800) 841-2222
www.cyclecountry.com

**Monroe-Tufline**
P.O. Box 186
Columbus, MS 39703
(662) 328-8347
www.monroetufline.com

**Country Home Products**
P.O. Box 25
Vergennes, VT 05491
(800) 699-2059
www.drfieldbrush.com

**Plotmaster**
Woods-N-Water, Inc.
311 North Marcus St.
Wrightsville, GA 31096
(478) 864-9108
www.theplotmaster.com

**Wildlife Specialty Products**
P.O. Box 1107
Yazoo City, MS 39194
(800) 748-9022
www.amcomfg.com

# CHAPTER 6

# TREE PLANTING
## COMES FIRST

Those who plant food plots soon develop many friendships. Likely as not, just within a few miles of where your property is situated, other sportsmen/landowners likewise have planted food plots for deer and other wildlife species. Making friends with them allows you to share experiences and learn from each other's mistakes and successes.

How do you find out about these individuals? Through your county extension agent! He's undoubtedly been in touch with them, to assist with their needs, knows where they're located and can help you make contact with them. The extension agent himself is likewise a fountain of information and over the years he'll probably be the first person you contact with questions. So it's beneficial to be on good terms with him. Invite him out to your place for coffee and to see your operation so you're on a first-name basis.

County extension agents deal primarily as a clearinghouse of information for landowners involved in all aspects of raising crops and livestock in that specific region, so there's a good deal of overlap in their expertise with food plots and wildlife. But also, you'll want to establish a relationship with your county Natural Resource Conservation Service office. The NRCS focuses primarily upon wise land-use practices in accordance with the topography and soil-types that predominate in that region.

There also are a number of private consulting agencies eager to help landowners. One of the newest, that's specifically devoted to food plots and deer management, is NorthCountry Whitetails which is based in New York State and run by a host of experts who are well known among sportsmen.

NORTHCOUNTRY WHITETAILS

**Every state has several agricultural-assistance agencies to help landowners. On the national scene, New York-based NorthCountry Whitetails specializes in land-management for deer. Here, their tram tours one of 20 food plot situations to show visitors how it's done.**

Their particular specialty is working with land managers in the northern half of the United States (north of South Carolina) and southern Canada.

NorthCountry Whitetails offers land managers a variety of seed products, reference materials and other supplies. But also, they offer a number of services; just one is soil-testing analysis, along with subsequent recommendations as to how to achieve a maximum return from your food plot plantings.

However, the most revolutionary concept developed by NorthCountry Whitetails is on-site consulting and professional advice to land managers. A representative will actually visit your property to advise on layout and deer forage plantings tailored specifically to your unique property holding. If you're a very busy person, the organization will even attend to your food plot planting projects from beginning to end, leaving you with a turn-key operation. Their fee is calculated on an hourly basis, plus expenses; in some cases this approach may be more cost-effective than doing the work yourself because you receive the assurance and peace of mind that the job is done right, the first time.

Since this concept is so new, I advise landowners first participate in one of the tours hosted by NorthCountry Whitetails at their 500-acre demo site in Stueben County, New York. The tour is very modestly priced and consists of a 6-hour program in which visitors ride a tram to over 20 locations on the property where you are shown first-hand how to transform property into high-quality wildlife habitat.

For more information, go to the organization's web site at www.northcountrywhitetails.com.

## BUT WHY PLANT TREES FIRST?

Just one of many educational services provided by NorthCountry Whitetails involves TSI. This acronym stands for "timber-stand improvement" and it involves several facets: The periodic, selective logging-off of mature timber that isn't beneficial to wildlife but can provide income to finance food plot projects; the corrective pruning of immature trees that are beneficial to wildlife or eventually will produce valuable timber; and, the removal of "scrub" tree species (hornbeam, sweet gum, black gum, sycamore, cottonwood) that have little wildlife or commercial value so that planted food plots can take their place. Also, in specific places where trees have been removed but food plots are not to be planted in their place, usually due to unsuitable terrain, new tree plantings should be undertaken.

This brings us back full-circle to the beginning of this chapter because, other than private nursery operations, there are two main sources of trees.

One is your county extension service, which works in cooperation with the forestry division of your state department of natural resources; a wide variety of hardwood and softwood seedling species are sold at nominal cost, often as low as a few cents apiece.

The other source of seedlings is your NRCS office which works in cooperation with large timber companies such as Weyerhauser, Westvaco, and Meade. Landowners are provided with tree seedlings, usually softwood conifer species, often free of cost.

In both cases, a simple order form is filled out in winter and trees are delivered in time for spring planting.

There are several reasons for a landowner to engage in tree planting as the first step in his wildlife habitat management program. First,

Certain hardwood species are more beneficial to deer than others, due to their mast production but also the animals' preference for browsing leaves and branchtips.

**It can take an oak 40 years before it begins producing a bountiful acorn crop relished by deer and turkeys, but that's no reason not to plant them. Being a good steward of the land means allocating 10 percent of your tree planting efforts to hardwoods "for the next generation."**

if he recently had timber removed from the land, he'll want to as quickly as possible stabilize the ground to prevent erosion and slippage; and the most common, and effective, way to do this is to plant new trees in place of those removed.

But also, even if you committed this very minute to launching upon a project of establishing food plots, you probably wouldn't be putting the first seed into the ground for at least a year. There will be needed equipment considerations to take care of, soil test samples to have analyzed, specific types of forages to be decided upon, seeds to be ordered, perhaps even terrain areas to be cleared of brush, and numerous consultation meetings to be had with various organizations and agencies for advice.

So during the meanwhile, whenever you have available time, is the perfect opportunity to plant trees. No significant investment is required or even special equipment other than a few basic hand tools. Moreover, as long as the ground is not frozen, tree planting can be done regardless of weather conditions, and the soil doesn't require any special preparation in advance.

Another reason for giving tree planting top priority is simply because trees take a long time to grow. So the sooner you begin, the better. In fact, it's been said that one plants trees not for himself but for the next generation. So strictly from a conservation standpoint, a good steward of the land allocates about 10 percent of his tree planting efforts to the valuable and important hardwood species. Oak trees in particular commonly live well over 100 years and can take 30 to 50 years before they begin producing mast and usable timber. As a result, long into the future, your children and their children will give silent thanks to you every time they marvel at those giants towering overhead.

Conversely, softwoods—the conifer species—grow rapidly, as much as four feet in height per year. And since they almost immediately begin producing a widespread, bushy conformation, they are important to all wildlife species in terms of shelterbelts offering protective hiding and nesting cover. They're also important to foodplots in terms of serving as windbreaks

## PLANTING HARDWOODS

Certain species of hardwoods are more beneficial to deer and wildlife than others, due to the mast (nuts or seeds) and succulent browse (leaves, twigs, buds) they produce. However, hardwoods are as unique to certain regions as the inhabiting wildlife species themselves, mostly as a result of the climate and soil conditions that predominate in those regions. That's why, regarding oaks living north of the Mason-Dixon line, the many members of the white oak family predominate, with deer specifically favoring the pin oak subspecies. Conversely, in the South we also see the white oak species but with deer preferring the swamp chestnut subspecies; in many regions of the South, an even higher percentage of oaks are the red and black oak varieties. So as a rule, good advice is to evaluate the predominant hardwood species on your specific property and plant those which are evident but scant in number or replace those removed during logging operations.

One exception to all of this is the sawtooth oak. It's somewhat of a dwarf oak species that, compared to other oaks which do best in deepwood's regions, thrives in open, sun-drenched spaces. Its most predominant feature, however, is that it produces mast (acorns) in only a fraction of the time required by the other oak species; sawtooths begin

In managing a hardwood forest, it's vital to learn how to identify the species that predominate on your land and their particular needs. Identification guidebooks are available in bookstores.

bearing bountiful mast crops in as little as only seven years and at full maturity may yield 1,500 pounds of acorns.

Although hardwood species can be purchased in balled form, in which the root mass is contained within a bushel of soil-medium and wrapped tightly with burlap or perforated ag-plastic, such trees are prohibitively expensive to purchase in large numbers; they're usually reserved for metropolitan landscaping purposes, not reforestation projects.

Consequently, a land manager will want to purchase hardwoods in seedling-form known as "whips" that are bare-root stock and average three feet in length; they're shipped in bundles of 10 and wrapped in heavy paper with the roots kept moist in a small quantity of damp peat moss. The same is true with other desirable hardwoods such as maple, black walnut, black cherry, and birch.

Enclosed with each bundle of trees ordered will be a pamphlet describing proper planting procedures for that particular species and what type of fertilizer (if any) should be added at a later time. Of special importance, be sure the planting site receives plenty of

Most land managers plant hardwoods as so-called "whips" that are bare-root stock up to five feet in length. Check them in winter for signs of browsing damage. If necessary, they can be protected with inexpensive plastic sleeves from a nursery; these are oaks which in several years will be thinned.

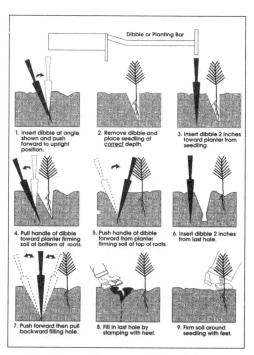

Dibble or Planting Bar

1. Insert dibble at angle shown and push forward to upright position.

2. Remove dibble and place seedling at correct depth.

3. Insert dibble 2 inches toward planter from seedling.

4. Pull handle of dibble toward planter firming soil at bottom of roots.

5. Push handle of dibble forward from planter firming soil at top of roots.

6. Insert dibble 2 inches from last hole.

7. Push forward then pull backward filling hole.

8. Fill in last hole by stamping with heel.

9. Firm soil around seedling with feet.

Conifer seedlings are sold in minimum bundles of 25 and are planted with a "dibble."

sunlight, and to retain habitat diversity don't crowd the trees; no more than ten per acre is sufficient.

The actual planting itself is quick and easy and makes use of a planting bar, or so-called "dibble," which is available at any farm-supply store; The planting method itself is the same as when planting softwoods and takes less than a minute per tree; see the diagram in this chapter.

The growth rate of hardwood species can be accelerated by fertilizing them every fall with one pound of 10-10-10 per inch of trunk diameter, measured at eye level. But don't simply dump it on the ground at the base of the trunk. With a pick, create a shallow trench (an inch or two deep) around the perimeter of the tree's drip line, pour the fertilizer evenly into it, then cover with the dirt formerly removed; the "drip-line" is the outermost edge of the overhead leaf canopy and is directly above the outermost area of the steadily expanding, underground root mass.

## PLANTING SOFTWOODS

Across the whitetail's range, the most common conifer species planted for wildlife cover and windbreaks are white pines, red pines, Austrian pines and loblolly pines. In select regions, various firs and spruces may also be available. Cedars are seldom available because of their low commercial value and because they are highly self-regenerating.

Pine seedlings are usually made available to landowners in lot quantities of 25 and packed in heavy paper with peat moss or ag-gel around the roots to keep them moist. With a dibble, they go into the ground fast; with just a few minutes of experience, anyone should be able to plant an average of 50 per hour.

With a bit of practice you can plant 50 conifers per hour. The area surrounding the base of the tree should be sprayed with herbicide the first year to prevent weed competition; note the handmade shield to protect the seedlings from the spray.

A series of diagrams in this chapter shows the proper method for planting conifers. But there's a very important aspect to keep in mind, and that is avoiding what's called J-rooting.

Conifer seedlings have a stringy root system that typically is longer than the planting hole created by the dibble. So if the seedling is inserted into the hole, as is, the lowermost tip of its root mass will often curl around in a J-shape, causing the roots to begin growing toward the surface; obviously, this kills the seedling. The easy remedy is to simply trim each seedling's root mass with

Conifers are planted in so-called "plantations" to serve as thick shelterbelts for wildlife cover, or as windbreaks to protect fragile food plots. Once established, a conifer seedling can grow four feet per year.

scissors or a knife so the roots are no more than 6 inches in length.

Conifers do well in acidic soil, but if the pH is lower than 6.0 a one-time lime-and-fertilizer application is beneficial to get the trees established; this involves merely dropping a special "tablet" in the dibble slot when the seedlings go into the ground; they're available at farm-supply stores.

Seedlings available for free from state agencies working in cooperation with timber companies generally are about six to eight inches in length. These are one-year-old seedlings and they're entirely satisfactory. But whenever possible, and if they're available, I prefer to pay a small extra amount to obtain three-year-old seedlings. They average 18 to 20 inches in length and since they have a more developed root-mass give you a several-year headstart in their growth rate. It's recommended that conifer seedlings be planted in so-called plantations—even rows with a minimum spacing of 8 feet between each tree and each row.

When serving as windbreaks around food plots, conifers should be planted in rectangular plantations consisting minimally of six to eight rows and they should be situated along the north, northwest, west and southwest sides of the food plots to give them a measure of protection from prevailing winds and storm systems. When serving as shelterbelts for wildlife, conifers should be planted in square blocks of at least ten rows, with most of these blocks, preferably, in lower-elevation areas where higher, surrounding hillsides also aid in protecting the habitat from strong winds and driving precipitation.

The first year after planting, it's wise to use a hand-sprayer to apply a herbicide to the ground-cover in an 18-inch swath around the base of each tree. This prevents competing weeds from growing higher than the seedlings, shading them out and causing them to become stunted. The most popular herbicide is Roundup, but this is not species-selective and will kill any plantlife it comes in contact with, including conifer seedlings. The easiest way to prevent this is to cut a three-foot length of scrap plastic pipe that's about four inches in diameter and attach some type of handle to one end. Then, as you walk down the row of your planted seedlings, lower the pipe over the top of each tree to entirely protect it from spray-drift; then simply lift the pipe and move on to the next seedling. The ground cover surrounding hardwood "whip" seedlings and balled/burlapped fruit trees does not have to be treated with herbicide; they're tall enough to not be shaded-out.

## FRUIT TREES

The most popular fruit trees among land managers targeting deer and other wildlife are common apple, crabapple, persimmon, pear, plum, and honeylocust. All three, when mature, bear an annual crop that is measured in tonnage.

Fruit trees for wildlife are never planted in large numbers. However, many varieties have both male and female characteristics and must have a "mate" of the same species within line-of-sight and no more than 100 yards away so insects may cross-pollinate them.

Apple trees, depending upon the species, bear fruit at various times beginning in midsummer and throughout the late fall. I like see a variety of trees on a given tract of land so that one or another is always a viable food source during this five-month time frame. Another characteristic of apple trees is that they drink enormous quantities of water; during their first two years in the ground, periods of extremely dry weather (during the spring-summer growing months) require giving them at least 5 gallons of water per week.

There are many mail-order nurseries that specialize in fruit trees (as well as hardwoods and softwoods) that are beneficial to deer and other wildlife; see the tree-source-listing at the end of this chapter. However, their one shortcoming is that their fruit trees typically consist of small, bare-root stock averaging 24 to 48 inches in length and take one or two years just to anchor their roots before they begin growing. I much prefer to buy larger fruit trees at local nurseries or garden shops in balled/burlapped form. Since fruit trees can be planted in either the spring or fall, if you get them late

When deciding upon planting sites for fruit trees, keep in mind they require enormous amounts of water and many species must have a "mate" within 100 yards for cross-pollination.

in the season they often are marked down to less than half price. These are trees that may be as much as ten feet tall and have root masses that can weigh 75 pounds or more, so transporting them to their planting sites require a four-wheeler or tractor frontloader.

Follow the planting instructions that come with each tree. Generally, the procedure involves digging a hole that is somewhat deeper and wider than the balled root mass, setting the tree in place, adding one-quarter pound of 10-10-10 fertilizer and then the fill dirt, and then implanting a stake of sorts with the tree tied to it by a rope to steady the tree in strong wind until it has had a full year to anchor its roots. Some of these tree species may begin bearing fruit within three years of planting, but their most bountiful crops are not borne until they are ten years or older.

## COMMERCIAL TREE SOURCES

**Heather Farms Nursery**
2961 King Rd.
Morrison, TN 37357
(800) 451-3889
www.hfnhomedirect.com

**Hillis Nursery Co.**
92 Gardner Rd.
McMinneville, TN 37110

**Mellinger's Nursery**
2310 W. South Range Road
North Lima, OH 44452
(800) 321-7444

**Musser Forest Inc.**
P.O. Box 340
Indiana, PA 15701
(412) 465-5685

**Southern Wildlife Products**
P.O. Box 489
Eufaula, AL 36072
(877) 813-8500
www.southern-wildlife.com

**Whitetail Institute of North America**
239 Whitetail Trail
Pintlala, AL 36043
(800) 688-3030
www.deernutrition.com

**The Wildlife Group**
2858 County Road 53
Tuskegee, AL 36083
(800) 221-9703
www.wildlifegroup.com

# CHAPTER 7

# CLOVERS AND CLOVER BLENDS
## FOR DEER

Is there any particular planted food that deer universally favor over all others? In my opinion, the answer is a resounding yes, and it's clover!

Is there any particular food that landowners especially like to plant for deer? Again, the answer is yes. Clover!

Deer like clover because it's highly nutritious and palatable. And those who plant food plots like clover because it's relatively easy to plant and it's perennial, so it doesn't have to be planted every year and this makes it less expensive than some other food plot choices.

Are there any disadvantages to clover? Sure. Keep in mind that one reason for

**Deer relish clover. And since it's easy to plant and maintain, that also makes it a favorite food plot choice among land managers.**

putting in any type of food plot is to attract and hold deer and other wildlife on your property by offering them something special that's not available elsewhere in their immediate home-range area. Unfortunately, if your neighbors who own surrounding property are also putting in numerous food plots planted to clover, or they're growing it for hay production for livestock, you won't accomplish much by planting it yourself.

This is a key element in deciding upon what to put into food plots. Whether we're talking about clover, corn, soybeans or any other food, always do a little covert research to learn what your neighbors are regularly planting, either as farm crops or food plots targeting specific wildlife species. Then, select forages that are highly nutritious and palatable but different than what everyone else in the immediate area is planting.

Okay then, let's say you've decided to plant clover. Sounds simple enough until one talks with an agronomist and we learn there are many clovers. In North America the most common varieties are red, white, crimson, arrowleaf, berseem, kenland, webfoot, millennium, and ladino.

To make the matter even more complicated, within various clover categories there are sub-varieties. For example, there are six varieties of ladino clover; they are arcadia, merit, osceola, sonja, tillman, and titan.

As might be expected, certain clovers do better than others in certain climates and soil conditions.

## A CLOSER LOOK

If a land manager, for whatever reason, should decide to plant a specific clover variety rather than a blend, he'll naturally want that particular clover to do as well as possible. Following are just a few characteristics of the more well-known and widely available clovers; your extension agent can provide still more information.

• **ARROWLEAF CLOVER** is highly favored by deer. It grows faster in spring than many other varieties, providing deer with a highly nutritious post-winter food source. It's adapted to a wide range of fertile, well-drained soil conditions that are mildly acid to mildly alkaline. It does best as a fall planting but it doesn't do as well as some other clovers in the colder, northern states.

• **CRIMSON CLOVER,** although regularly eaten by deer, is particularly favored by turkeys. It favors fertile, well-drained soils and does best as a fall planting. It is not cold-hardy enough for most northern states.

• **LADINO CLOVER,** a proprietary variety, is highly favored by deer. It's also highly favored by landowners across the whitetail's range because of its disease resistance and winter hardiness. It does best as a spring planting.

• **MILLENNIUM CLOVER** is highly favored by deer but difficult to establish. It starts out slow and is barely evident the first year of planting. But once established, it grows thick, spreads rapidly and lasts ten years or longer; as a result, to avoid having a barren food plot the first year, it should be co-planted with some other grass forage such as trefoil. Millenium clover is winter hardy, drought-resistant and tolerates a wide range of soil conditions. A spring seeding is recommended.

• **OSCEOLA CLOVER** is eagerly sought by deer. It does best as a late-spring planting. However, this particular ladino variety experiences extensive damage when temperatures plummet below freezing, so it's best reserved for southern landowners or those who live in warm coastal regions.

Of the many clover varieties, deer prefer ladino. But the Whitetail Institute of North America has formulated a blend of this and numerous other clovers, called Imperial Whitetail, that better meet a wide variety of growing conditions.

• **RED CLOVER** is highly preferred by deer. It adapts to a wide variety of soil types and does better on sandy soils than most other clovers. It does best as a fall planting. Its main disadvantage is that, unlike some other clovers that may remain viable for four to six years, red clover is a biannual; after only two years it begins to fade out and must be replanted, thereby making it a more expensive clover food plot option than some other plantings.

• **WEBFOOT CLOVER** is extremely preferred by deer, waterfowl and small game such as rabbits. As its name implies, it is especially well-adapted to fertile, wet lowlands and swampy areas that quickly "puddle" during rainy periods and afterward never seem to entirely dry out. Planting in late summer is recommended.

• **WHITE CLOVER** is moderately preferred by deer, turkeys and quail and adapts well to a wide variety of soil types except those which are extremely dry or wet. It does best as a fall planting. Its main advantage is that it's a long-lived perennial.

## GO WITH THE CLOVER BLENDS

According to test results by the Whitetail Institute of North America, which serves as a central clearinghouse of research information devoted exclusively to the whitetail deer, the particular clover most preferred by deer are those in the ladino family. However, in terms of improving the overall health of the species and greatly enhancing antler growth, and doing well under a wide variety of growing conditions, any of the ladinos should be blended with several other strains.

That's why Alabama-based WINA, spearheaded by Ray Scott, developed its own clover blend for those who plant food plots, and they call it Imperial Whitetail Clover.

I was thinking about this one day while looking down upon one of my small food plots from a nearby tree stand. Below me were four does and two bucks and whenever they periodically turned at just the right angle to the early morning sunlight their coats glistened like neon signs. Even more impressive, both bucks sported larger antlers than we customarily see in southeastern Ohio.

W.I.N.A.

At W.I.N.A. research grounds, their Imperial Whitetail Clover blend has been found to yield 25- to 35-percent protein content, which is far more than alfalfa and other livestock grass forages.

"The reason the deer appeared to shine was because of lanolin in their coats," biologist friend Larry Weishuhn explained, "and this, along with the larger than average antlers, was due to an abundance of body mineral the deer can't usually obtain from native forage alone."

In recent years, Ray Scott, Larry Weishuhn and many others have been intently studying the dietary needs of deer and the conclusions they've reached are startling the outdoor world. "When deer are forced to get by with whatever nature provides, they are continually in a survival-mode," Weishuhn explains. "But when sportsmen-landowners enter the picture and begin providing deer with plenty of extras, trophy bucks are the result."

To satisfy their nutritional needs, whitetails require about seven pounds of bulk food intake per day. Yet the big mistake made by hunters and landowners is providing food plot sustenance only in the spring and summer when deer need help the least. Instead, they should be helping deer during the worst of times.

This is critically important because it must be remembered that nutritional intake goes first to meet basic survival needs of an individual deer. It is only after these metabolic requirements are met do excess nutrients find themselves channeled into disease resistance, muscular and skeletal development, fawn development and milk production in does, and antler growth in bucks. Now you know why, some years, does in a given region have only single fawns and most of the bucks have thin, spindly antlers; the previous winter was particularly hard on them and their body metabolisms commandeered virtually all spring and summer nutrient intake just to return them to a state of normal body health.

Consequently, when a given region is not producing large numbers of deer, and few quality bucks, it's almost always because nutritional foods are available there only on a seasonal basis.

"This is exactly why I got involved in the development of Imperial Whitetail Clover," Ray Scott says. "Most quality grass forages used for hay production (such as alfalfa, lespedeza and birdsfoot trefoil) have a 16- to 18-percent protein content, but the clover blend we designed has an average of 25- to 35-percent protein!"

But why blend together numerous clover species? The reason is because, as noted earlier, each has its own environmental strengths and weaknesses. Some clover strains are better able to withstand drought conditions than others, some tolerate unusually wet seasons very well, others are better adapted to abnormal heat spells while still others flourish during periods of prolonged cool temperatures. In yet other cases, some strains seem to do better in sandy soils while others are better suited to clay soils, and some clover varieties are more disease and insect resistant than others.

As a result, if a landowner plants a clover blend rather than a single variety, he's virtually assured a lush food plot because the combined superior traits of the individual clovers comprising the blend will each contribute their attributes and allow the overall stand to do well under the prevailing weather or soil conditions at a given time or in a given location.

Equally significant—and this goes back to our earlier mention of the importance of deer receiving highly nutritional food on a year-around basis—Imperial Whitetail Clover does not turn as "woody" and stemmy in late summer and does not as quickly brown-out and go dormant in winter like many other grass forages. Although Imperial Whitetail Clover, like all vegetation, dramatically slows down in growth in bitter cold winter weather, and eventually goes into a dormant state, its protein level lasts all year. Moreover, its blended components adapt to a wide range of soil conditions and it does not require annual reseeding, so these attributes make it an ideal food plot consideration throughout most of the U.S. and southern Canada.

Incidentally, still another attribute of Imperial Whitetail Clover is that it does well in semi-shaded areas. So if a landowner chooses, he can reserve this particular food for his deeper woodland regions and plant other selected foods in areas which receive greater daily sunlight exposure.

Imperial Whitetail Clover does especially well in moist, fertile soil. Consequently, WINA similarly developed ALFA-RACK, which is a special clover-alfalfa blend for drier, well-drained soil; it's discussed more thoroughly in the next chapter.

Moreover, WINA blends are fine-tuned for each customer in accordance with how far north he lives. This is a first in the industry; when you call to order Imperial or ALFA-RACK, the company's computer uses your zip code to determine which specific blend of either product is sent to you.

"As far as palatability, deer prefer Imperial Whitetail Clover and ALFA-RACK 5-to-1 over cattle-type grasses," says Scott. "On our research grounds, the clover literally sucks deer out of surrounding regions. They frequently walk right through other food plots to reach it."

What is even more noteworthy than Imperial Whitetail Clover's ability to draw deer from afar is the effect it has upon antler growth. On the Whitetail Institute of North America's research grounds, where deer had the opportunity to dine upon this unique clover blend over a brief period of only 4 years, the occurrence of spike bucks entirely disappeared! Every 18 month old buck sporting his first "hard" antlers had a six-point rack or better!

Such results are based upon the sound biological principle that when deer are nutritionally well-fed on a year-around basis, they do not find themselves subjected to a spring recovery period. There's no required bounce-back time to compensate for winter's toll. And this means that when spring arrives, does may immediately get on with the business of birthing and nursing healthy twins and triplets, and bucks may immediately begin laying down a foundation for heavy antler growth.

Imperial Whitetail Clover is now available at leading seed and farm supply dealers. If you can't find it in your region, it can be purchased directly from WINA and shipped via UPS.

## OTHER CLOVER BLENDS

With the rapid growth in the nationwide popularity of planting food plots for deer and other wildlife, literally dozens of seed companies have sprouted and each month advertise heavily in sportsmen's magazines, farm journals and on the internet.

But be wary. Many such companies are located in the deep South and that's where their research and product development has taken place. As a result, in a great many cases their clover blends and other forage products are specifically tailored to southern soils and climates where those plantings do quite well. Yet as the research specialists at New York-based NorthCountry Whitetails are fond of saying, "When your winter food plots look more like hockey rinks than botanical gardens, different products and strategies are called for."

Consequently, if you live north of the Mason-Dixon Line, it's always a wise practice, when deciding upon clovers or clover blends for your own food plots, to first carefully read the product literature available from various companies before investing time and money in any planting effort.

Many companies, in their literature, print a nationwide map with designated climate zones where their products have been proven to do well, and also the time-frames when their clovers should be planted in those regions. In the case of clover blends, they also list the individual clover varieties comprising their particular formulation. It's wise to then consult with your county extension agent or NRCS office regarding the feasibility of planting that particular blend in your area; although the climate may be suitable, the specific soil-type in your immediate area may not.

## SPRING PLANTING

Some clovers and blends such as ladino, millennium and Imperial Whitetail Clover are best suited to spring planting. But first, when a land manager has decided to put one or more food plots into a clover or blend purchased from a company engaged in research dealing with wildlife forages, I strongly recommend requesting their video-tape that gives planting instructions. Nowadays there are so many wildlife forages available, so many food plot blends, and so many companies marketing these products, that providing here detailed planting instructions on each is beyond the scope of this book. So first read the literature available from various companies and after deciding which specific plantings are of interest to you, then view their videos to learn beforehand what's involved in terms of equipment, time, or other considerations.

Clover food plots require a well-prepared seedbed, but the first and most important consideration is applying a herbicide to avoid later weed competition that can ruin a plot. This eight-foot boom sprayer quickly mounts on the back of any ATV.

As a broad overview, one of the greatest mistakes landowners make in putting in a clover food plot is simply plowing and/or disking a weedfield and then planting the seed. Although much of the clover (or other forage) will germinate and grow, it will quickly become overrun with weeds due to the billions of weedseeds turned under.

Much wiser is to first use a non-specific, systemic herbicide such as Round-Up or Arsenal, or an Atrazine-Princep blend that is both systemic and prevents dormant weedseeds from germinating, to eliminate the clover's competition. If you have any doubts or questions about this planting phase, consult your county extension agent. And of course, as we saw in a previous chapter, the ground should have been limed many months earlier to allow the mineral to become absorbed by the soil. About ten days after the ground has been treated with the herbicide, and the weeds are now non-existent, the ground should next see the application of fertilizer in accordance with the soil-test recommendations.

Then and only then should the intended food plot area be plowed and/or harrow-disked so that it's ready for planting. But don't immediately plant! For the highest possible germination rate, soil moisture is critical. Therefore, a rule that applies to virtually any farming operation is this: Never plant in dry soil and hope for rain! Instead, prepare the soil and then begin monitoring not only your local weather forecasts but also the storm-front conditions on a national weather map. When the time is right, and mild but steady precipitation is predicted to arrive within 72 hours, that's the time to plant.

As to actual planting techniques, establishing clover food plots is not difficult because the seeds are quite small and therefore do not need to be set deeply or covered with much soil.

As a standard rule of thumb, any type of seed—even that which goes into a common home vegetable garden—should be planted at a depth of approximately four-times the length of the seed.

As a result, small seeds such as clover, which are not much larger than a pinhead, should be planted only 1/8- to 1/4-inch deep. With a fine-textured soil it's not even necessary to "bury" the seeds; many land managers simply broadcast-spread the seed with a shoulder-bag/hand-crank seeder or ATV-mounted cyclone-spreader and then go over the ground with a drag-roller or cultipacker to simply press the seeds into the surface of the soil. Although it takes longer, simply spreading

Since clover seeds are tiny, they aren't "planted" in the traditional sense but simply pressed into the soil surface. With the Plotmaster, this is accomplished with a rear drag roller.

the seed and then driving over it with an ATV, tractor or truck will accomplish the same end; the tires pressing downward cause good seed contact with the soil without deeply burying the seed.

Clover-seeding rates range from 12 to 20 pounds per acre, depending upon the variety or blend. Of special importance is that most clovers and blends are legumes that must be inoculated prior to planting. An inoculant is a powdery seed coating that facilitates germination; it comes in a small, several-ounce bag and is simply mixed in with the seed, by hand, just prior to planting. As a selling point, many seed companies pre-inoculate their clovers to save the landowner a bit of time.

## MAINTAINING CLOVER FOOD PLOTS

Although there are exceptions, most clovers and clover-blend food plots usually remain viable for three to five years before re-seeding becomes necessary. Nevertheless, visually inspecting your plots on a regular basis is important. If after several years you see a slow, uniform degradation of the plot, it's usually an indication the clover is nearing the end of its life cycle and you should begin thinking about re-seeding that fall or the following spring.

However, if the clover plot is a relatively new planting and is degrading but only in random places, it may only be experiencing a lime or fertilizer deficiency in those "spotty" locations. So before investing the time and money in complete re-seeding, have a quick, inexpensive soil-test sample analyzed to gain more information. Then, hand broadcast-spread the recommended lime or fertilizer to re-invigorate those locations.

It should also be mentioned that even with a herbicide application prior to planting it's impossible to completely elimi-nate weeds from food plots; you may kill those weeds and deac-tivate those seeds that initially were present in the soil just prior to

When using a tractor-pulled implement to seed clover, a cultipacker uniformly sets the seeds just 1/4-inch deep.

planting but the effects of "wind-drift" will slowly but steadily repopulate your plots from adjacent acreage.

Therefore, once or twice a year, it's wise to mow your clover food plots for the purpose of reducing any weed growth that is almost sure to begin competing with your clover for soil nutrients, moisture, sunlight, and space.

A bush-hog of sorts, pulled behind a tractor or ATV, is commonly used, with the primary aim being to either kill annual broadleaf weed species or at least prevent them from multiplying by cutting them off below their seeding point; otherwise, if the weeds are permitted to re-seed themselves, they'll eventually take over the food plot.

The best time to mow food plots planted to clovers or clover blends is when they reach a height of 8 inches, so that the remaining stand is about 5 inches in height; this practice not only controls weeds but also stimulates rapid regrowth of the clover.

In wet years, you may have to mow two or three times. However, avoid mowing during periods of extremely hot weather, or during droughts, when all forms of vegetation are in a state of stress.

If any of your clover food plots are more than two acres in size, an attractive alternative to mowing them yourself is to invite a neighbor farmer to not only mow them for you but also rake and bale the resulting "hay" that he can use for livestock feed. If he offers to do the work and to additionally pay for the hay taken away on a per-bale basis, that's terrific because the cash-flow will help defray your other land-management expenses. But even if your neighbor doesn't care to pay for the hay, it's still to your benefit; simply having him do the required mowing saves the time and expense of doing it yourself.

There's still another option that's highly attractive to land managers (and deer) in the northernmost states where severe winter weather can greatly reduce available wildlife forage. Instead of inviting a neighbor farmer to "take off" your clover as hay for his livestock, pay him to cut and bale the forage for you. Or do it on a "shares" basis in which he performs the labor and takes three-quarters of the crop and gives you the remaining quarter. This is an especially wise practice if your food plots are in a clover blend or other high quality perennial grass such as alfalfa. Later in the year winter, the resulting hay bales can then be intermittently delivered to various places on your property via four-wheeler, their string ties cut and the forage scattered on the ground to supplementally feed deer and other wildlife. Ideally, the hay bales should be stored until needed in some type of weatherproof barn or shed, but they can also be stored in the open if covered with large nylon tarps securely anchored around their perimeters.

Weed control not done by mowing can also be accomplished by spraying the food plots with a herbicide but you'll want to use a selective chemical that targets only unwanted grasses and broadleaf plants. In taking this approach, be sure to consult with your county extension agent because purchasing and using some herbicide brands requires an applicator's license; obtaining such a license requires studying a herbicide-usage manual and taking a proficiency test.

Again I'd like to emphasize using caution with any type of herbicide by thoroughly reading the labeling safety instructions. Then, study the application rates because too little herbicide will not eradicate the weeds and too much can kill the clover. Then, read the safety precautions again!

## FALL CLOVER PLANTINGS

If, for some reason, it was not possible to plant a clover food plot in the spring, or it was a particular clover variety or blend that does better when planted later in the fall or early-winter period (depending upon latitude), keep one cardinal rule in mind: In timing your planting, most clovers and blends need a full six weeks after germination in order to survive winter periods characterized by frozen surface-ground as this allows them sufficient time to sufficiently bury their root systems.

In fact, fall seeding of many food plot forages has distinct advantages over spring seeding. The ground in spring often is too wet to prepare and if plowed or disked in this condition often results in large, hard clumps of soil rather than a fine seedbed. After spring planting, and before germination, too much rain can even cause seeds to rot in the ground. Conversely, the fall and early winter months usually (but not always) see only moderate rainfall, near-perfect soil temperature, and the emerging plants are more succulent than those which have been growing throughout the summer; as a result, during the fall/winter hunting seasons, a new fall-planted clover plot will invariably attract more deer and other wildlife than an earlier spring-planted food plot.

To ensure maximum germination, I like to hand-broadcast or machine-spread the seed using the equipment's smallest seed setting and going over the ground in one direction. Then I go over the ground a second time, going in a crosswise direction, to ensure a full and uniform distribution of seed.

Finally, the seed is barely pressed into the worked soil with a cultipacker or field roller; you can even use a six-foot-square of chain-link fence pulled behind an ATV, just like dragging the infield of a baseball diamond. Of course, everything previously said about soil test samples, liming and weed-arresting measures apply to fall planting the same as spring seeding.

So-called "over-seeding," in which seed is broadcast-spread on top of frozen ground covered with light snow is also sometimes done with clover and clover blends. However, since this is more commonly done with other legumes such as alfalfa, it's covered in the next chapter.

## CLOVER & CLOVER-BLEND SOURCES

**Adams-Briscoe Seed Co.**
P.O. Box 19
Jackson, GA 30233
(770) 775-7826
abseed@juno.com

**Hard Hunter Forage Blends**
1562 - 160th St.
Centuria, WI 54824
(800) 700-9334
www.hardhunter.com

**BioLogic**
P.O. Box 757
West Point, MS 39773
(601) 494-8859
www.mossyoak.com

**Texas Seed Co.**
221 Airport Blvd.
Kenedy, TX 78119
(800) 321-5673

**Whitetail Institute of North America**
Route 1, Box 3006
Pintlala, AL 36043
(800) 688-3030
www.deernutrition.com

# CHAPTER 8

# ALFALFA

## & OTHER PERENNIAL GRASSES

Many farmers across the country not-too-kindly refer to whitetails as "alfalfa bales wrapped in deer hide."

So this perennial legume pretty well describes one of the whitetail's favorite menu items. Plus, in addition to alfalfa's palatability, it has a nutritional value almost as high as the ladino clovers.

Yet as emphasized earlier, with regard to any food plot choices a landowner might be considering, alfalfa is a "boom or bust" proposition that depends upon what his neighbors already have in their own croplands or food plots. If alfalfa is popular in your specific region, planting this legume yourself will have little impact upon the whereabouts or feeding tendencies of deer and other wildlife. Conversely, if alfalfa is not extensively grown in your region, it will attract and hold far more deer than currently are on your acreage; it's also eagerly sought by turkeys, rabbits and geese.

Farmers are painfully aware of the whitetail's liking for alfalfa, which is exactly why it's a popular food plot planting among wildlife managers. Just make sure your neighbors aren't planting it as well.

"Alfalfa" actually is a generic name and, as with clovers, there are several varieties; apollo, vanguard, Florida 77, and forever alfalfa are the most common. The most popular and widely available commercial brand is known as Alfagraze.

## PLANTING ALFALFA

Preparing the ground for an alfalfa planting is very similar to doing so for a clover or a clover blend, so the reader may want to review that chapter. However, there are several exceptions that are important for the grower to keep in mind.

First, the fact that alfalfa is a legume means it has the ability to "fix" most of the nitrogen it needs by extracting it from the air and attaching it to its root nodules.

Of course, you'll want to first have a soil sample of the intended alfalfa-planting area sent to a lab for analysis. In so doing, you'll undoubtedly learn that periodic fertilizer applications at any time do not require a high nitrogen content; in fact, a common alfalfa fertilizer blend (revealing no nitrogen content whatever) is 0-20-20.

One soil component alfalfa does need, nearly always in greater amounts than other forage plantings, is lime. Alfalfa does not do well at all in acidic soil and needs a pH range of at least 6.7 to 7.0. So once again, allow your soil test sample to be your guide. And remember, as we emphasized in Chapter 4, lime should be applied to the ground and lightly disked into the soil at least four months before the seed is planted, to give the lime enough time to break down and become absorbed into the medium where it can be efficiently used as soon as the seeds germinate.

Alfalfa requires fertile, well-drained soil and therefore does not do well in many deep-south regions; however, where the soil is indeed suitable, alfalfa commonly is planted from early September

Alfalfa is planted the same as clover, but with one exception. Since it has a much deeper tap root, the ground must first be deep-plowed. An alternative to hiring-out this work is using a chisel attachment pulled behind a tractor or ATV.

until mid-October. But north of the Mason-Dixon line, it is commonly planted in either spring or fall, during the same time frames that the clover varieties are planted. All alfalfa strains, except forever alfalfa, have an average lifespan of three to four years before reseeding is recommended.

Forever alfalfa is a "new kid on the block" that is rapidly gaining favor. As its name implies, forever alfalfa (well, it's not really "forever") has a much longer lifespan than the other varieties. It extends its survival rate by means of a unique regenerative capability in which individual plants send out rhizomes (lateral, underground stems) from which new plants grow in a four-foot radius around the mother plant. Consequently, in a food plot, new plants are continually forming to replace the slowly aging and dying parents.

As mentioned in the previous chapter, when planting clover or any of the clover blends, which generally have a fibrous and shallow root system, breaking the ground with only a disk or combination harrow-disk usually is sufficient. But alfalfa has a deeper tap-root system and this means that, ideally, the ground should first be plowed. If you don't care to do conventional

Since alfalfa is a legume, it must be inoculated to facilitate germination. Some brands require the buyer to do this himself by mixing a powdery inoculant with the seed; instead, if possible, buy an alfalfa brand that is pre-inoculated by the seed company.

deep-plowing yourself, hire out the work to a neighbor farmer. Or, as an alternative, use a shallower-running chisel plow, or harrow-disk the ground twice, with the ground-breaking equipment pulled behind a small tractor or ATV. In any of these situations, as with clover, strive to achieve a seedbed that is as smooth, finely granulated and firm as possible.

A typical alfalfa planting calls for about 20 pounds of seed per acre, and using coated, pre-inoculated seed is recommended. However, unlike the clover varieties, alfalfa seed is planted a bit deeper; about 1/2-inch deep. Also unlike clover, the soil should be more firmly packed for a tighter soil-seed adhesion. This typically means broadcast spreading the seed and then going over the ground at least once, but preferably twice, with a cultipacker or heavy ground roller of sorts.

## MAINTAINING ALFALFA FOOD PLOTS

As with clover, alfalfa should periodically be mowed to reduce competition from weed growth. The best time to mow is when 25 percent of the alfalfa plants begin coming into bloom, but never cut it closer than three inches to the ground. In the northern states, the last mowing of the season should be timed in such a manner that the alfalfa stand is able to regain a growth-height of at least eight inches before the first killing frost.

Weed growth that gets out of control can also be dealt with by applying a selective, post-emergent herbicide; consult with your extension agent to learn which specific weed species are the problem and which particular herbicide he recommends. In any case, try to purchase the recommended herbicide in a so-called "rain-fast" variation. Since post-emergent herbicides are systemic, meaning they are absorbed by the plant and kill it internally all the way down to the root system, they ordinarily require 24 to 48 hours to begin working. If it unexpectedly rains during that time frame, the herbicide washes off and your time and money investment is wasted. Conversely, a rain-fast herbicide requires only 2 hours of drying time on the plants; if it rains any time after that, the herbicide is not diluted or washed off.

The one nemesis of all alfalfa strains, including those found in companion blends with various clovers, is the alfalfa weevil. If allowed to go unchecked, the insect can eventually devastate an alfalfa planting. Periodic mowing helps to keep weevils down, but some years a pesticide spray application may be called for. Since there are several species of weevils indige-

NORTHCOUNTRY WHITETAILS

When an alfalfa stand begins to thin, over-seeding in winter can extend its life
by another year or two.

nous to various regions, and different types of pesticides that work best on each, and different application strengths, this subject is one in which the landowner should consult with his local county extension agent.

In going back to seeding recommendations, one method that is particularly well-suited to legumes such as alfalfa is known as over-seeding. It's most commonly done north of the Mason-Dixon line during the winter months when the ground is frozen and there is snow-cover. This is an interim planting method to be undertaken when the legume stand is beginning to age but may have a year or two left if simply revitalized and upgraded but otherwise not requiring the landowner to engage in ground-breaking and replanting from scratch.

A shoulder-bag/hand-crank seed spreader is recommended and the land manager simply walks a methodical pattern back and forth across the food plot areas to be spot-planted; the snow itself allows you to see your seed being dispensed so that an even distribution over target areas is achieved.

The seed gradually sinks down through the snow, aided in time by additional snowfall on top, until it reaches the frozen ground. When the ground eventually begins to thaw, the seed next percolates into the top layer of the soil; as the soil eventually warms in the spring, the seed then germinates. Once the new plants are well-established, a top-dressing of fertilizer is recommended at a rate of 300 pounds of 0-20-20 per acre.

## CONSIDER PLANTING ALFA-RACK

Alfa-Rack is the brainchild of the Whitetail Institute of North America (WINA) that also produces the superior food plot blend known as Imperial Whitetail Clover. While Imperial Clover is the ideal choice for good quality soil that holds water, many landowners have property areas that don't retain

moisture well. The most common example is terrain that's high in clay or shale content, or slopes at more than ten degrees and therefore is prone to quick run-off of rainwater. In other cases, it's hardscrabble . . . infertile dirt with a low humus content and riddled with gravel and rocks.

One solution is Alfa-Rack, a blend of several alfalfa varieties that are high in protein, palatability,

Alfa-Rack, formulated by W.I.N.A., is a specialty blend of alfalfa and clover that is cold-weather tolerant and also does well in low-quality soils and during droughts.

7 5

Orchard grass is popular with many land managers because it grows well in shaded areas, making it an ideal choice for small food plots in deep-forest openings and grassy woodland trails.

longevity, and also have a high tolerance level for cold weather, droughty periods and low quality soils.

As mentioned earlier, virtually all alfalfa strains have a deep tap-root system, and this includes Alfa-Rack. But the Alfa-Rack blend also contains several varieties of clover that are shallow-rooted to take advantage of soil moisture that is destined to quickly run-off. As a result of this marriage, the clover component "fills in" to result in a food plot that remains lush, tender and palatable during adverse conditions and long after a pure alfalfa stand has become stemmy and hardened-off.

As with Imperial Whitetail Clover, WINA matches the consumer's zip code with the particular Alfa-Rack blend shipped to him so that it's just right for his climate zone.

## OTHER PERENNIAL GRASS PLANTINGS

Other food plot plantings commonly include American jointvetch, crownvetch, orchard grass, ryegrass, triticale, and birdsfoot trefoil. There are still dozens of others a landowner might also consider, either alone or in blended form, but these are the most popular among those who are specifically targeting the management of deer.

The immediate question that arises is this: If alfalfa, clovers, and blends of both, are of such high nutritional value and palatability to deer, why plant anything else?

The simple answer goes back to what we've emphasized before and that is the goal of providing deer with not only forages that are nutritious and palatable but to likewise attract and hold wildlife on your property. Consequently, you'll not want to focus your time, energy and financial resources upon alfalfa and clover if that's what's already growing on the other properties surrounding yours.

## AMERICAN JOINTVETCH

An interesting finding at Louisiana State University is that American jointvetch can change deer feeding behavior. Hunters know that whitetails, particularly mature bucks, like to feed during the low light levels of dawn and dusk. Yet American jointvetch draws them into food plots during midday because that's when sugar levels in this particular legume peak, making it especially tender and palatable.

American jointvetch also provides high protein levels for deer, and through the fall and winter months the plants' seeds are eagerly sought by turkeys, ducks, doves and quail.

Since American jointvetch is not cold-tolerant, it does best south of the Mason-Dixon line. It's generally planted from April through June and in the same manner as clover, with a seeding rate of 15 pounds per acre; Since it's a volunteer species, it reseeds itself, but the landowner can accelerate this process by disking the soil in early spring beginning with the second year after its initial seeding.

The species is unique in that it grows best in moist, well-drained sandy or clay soils that are quite acidic and have a pH of 5.0 to 6.0. Moreover, although American jointvetch is a legume, it can't fix as much nitrogen as it needs on its own and must receive supplemental feeding through a fertilizer application; a popular blend is 20-5-10 at planting time and 8-24-24 every year thereafter, spread at a rate of 250 pounds per acre. In a protected environment, American jointvetch can grow to a height of 7 feet tall, but in small food plots deer commonly keep it well grazed.

## CROWNVETCH

Crownvetch grows literally worldwide and spreads by seeds, stolens and rhizomes. It's often used for landscape beautification because it spreads as a permanent ground cover and thereby chokes out weeds. On behalf of wildlife, it's a beneficial food source frequently used by deer, quail and mourning doves. In all other regards, planting and fertilizing is the same as with American jointvetch.

## ORCHARD GRASS

Orchard grass is a perennial that will survive many years in both southern and northern states. It's a grass that thrives in the cooler months of the year, grows in clumps, and is commonly planted in combination with legumes or other forages such as wheat.

Although orchard grass in itself is not as eagerly sought as many other forages, its main attraction among land managers is that it's very shade tolerant. So it's a top consideration for those small, deep-forest openings, woodland trails and similar places where it's difficult to obtain a good stand of some other forage due to limited sunlight penetration through the overhead canopy.

Orchard grass is usually planted anytime from late March through September. It's seeded the same as clover at a rate of 5 pounds per acre, most often blended with equal quantities of winter wheat, spring wheat or even any leftover clover or alfalfa from previous spring plantings elsewhere. Although orchard grass does not require a high soil pH, it's usually wise to add lime anyway due to the lower pH levels required of the companion forages. Orchard grass does, however, require more nitrogen than most other forages and so a blend of 13-13-13 is suggested at a rate of 300 pounds per acre.

## RYEGRASS

Ryegrass is high on a deer's preferred forage list and is commonly planted by land managers because it serves a dual purpose. In addition to its palatability and high protein content, it's a dense growing, sod-forming grass that achieves rapid growth in early spring and quickly spreads. Consequently, it's an ideal planting for low to moderate quality soils that are highly erosion-prone such as steep, spotty, bare-dirt hillsides, woodland trails, and other terrain where, otherwise, only weed species would grow. Sometimes also known as Marshall grass, ryegrass is seeded the same as clover but since it's quite cold-hardy it's usually planted in late fall or early winter; the recommended seeding rate is 30 pounds per acre. A soil pH of 6.0 is required, so have a soil sample analyzed. Fertilizing rate is usually about 400 pounds of triple-13 per acre and it should be split; that is, half applied to the ground at planting time in the fall and the second half applied the following spring.

Many land managers targeting deer in particular blend 100 pounds of winter peas (per acre) with their ryegrass.

## TRITICALE

Triticale is another popular deer forage that serves the dual purpose of thwarting land-slippage in erosion-prone areas. Triticale is available in both spring and fall varieties. In the

**In food plot areas that are erosion-prone and too steep to use a tractor or ATV, triticale is a popular planting among deer and land managers alike. Simply "walk in" a garden tiller to rough-up the ground to at least 1 inch deep.**

Deer love birdsfoot trefoil and it's a versatile planting option because it's very winterhardy but also tolerates poor soil and heat. A sub-variety called junkyard trefoil is an ideal patch kit that can be easily broadcast over-seeded in existing grass or legume plantings that are beginning to thin.

South, I recommend using the spring variety and planting it in early April. North of the Mason-Dixon line I recommend using the fall variety and planting it in late August; the fall variety has the same cold tolerance as ryegrass.

The suggested seeding rate of triticale is 100 pounds per acre. However, unlike most other forage choices a land manager might consider, triticale is typically planted much deeper.

Since one-inch deep is the recommended seeding depth, and since the erosion-prone terrain to be planted usually is sloping and not conducive to the use of tractor- or ATV-operation, I use a common garden tiller to break up the ground. Then, after broadcast spreading the seed, I hand-rake the soil to cover it. This makes a triticale planting more laborious than most others, but thankfully the erosion-prone ground usually is small and the land steward can accomplish two goals at once; achieving a green forage source in winter and stabilizing the problem terrain area.

Triticale is rather fussy when it comes to fertilizer, particularly with the nitrogen component, so in the case of larger plantings (more than 1 acre) have a soil sample analyzed; in the case of large plantings, or those in small, spotty locations, a 13-6-8 fertilizer is suggested, and broadcast-spreading by hand usually is sufficient.

## BIRDSFOOT TREFOIL

Birdsfoot trefoil tests up to 34 percent protein and is especially popular with landowners in northern climates because it's very winterhardy. It also tolerates low soil-fertility levels and soils that have a low pH and poor drainage characteristics.

By description, trefoil is a perennial legume that looks almost identical to alfalfa but has finer stems and more leaves, resulting in a forage that remains lush even during hot, dry weather. It's generally planted, north and south, in August and September and in the same manner as alfalfa and clover but at a seeding rate of only 10 pounds per acre.

Birdsfoot trefoil has a longer lifespan than all other legumes and will remain viable up to ten years if fertilized annually with 5-14-42 at a rate of 250 pounds per acre.

Hamann Farms in Mason, Wisconsin is the country's leading supplier of birdsfoot trefoil and their two most popular varieties are Grower and Fall Deer Blend. The Grower variety provides the highest protein level in spring and summer when antler development is crucial and fawns are nursing. The Fall Deer Blend consists of two varieties of trefoil, three high-protein clovers, canola, winter rye and perennial rye, resulting in a very high cold-weather blend that produces a lush greenfield late into the winter.

A sub-variety of trefoil is junkyard trefoil, a perennial legume that grows in the most extreme conditions. It easily tolerates poor soil, drought, heat, and cold winter weather, remaining tender and delicate all the while. Junkyard trefoil will fill in, grow and persist in spotty places of large food plots where nothing else will grow. You don't even need to lime and fertilize it, and deer nevertheless relish it!

I use junkyard trefoil as a quick "patch kit" wherever an intended forage planting has been spotty and I just haven't had time to analyze and correct the problem. Or I use it as a stop-gap whenever I want to quickly develop a long-term food plot in a particular area but haven't yet decided what to plant there but want something growing for the deer as quickly as possible.

## ALFALFA AND PERENNIAL GRASS SEED SOURCES

**Adams-Briscoe Seed Co.**
P.O. Box 19
Jackson, GA 30233
(770) 775-7826
abseed@juno.com

**C.M. Payne & Son, Inc.**
9410 Payne Rd.
Sebring, FL 33872
(941) 385-4642

**C.P. Daniel's Son, Inc.**
P.O. Box 119
Waynesboro, GA 30830
(800) 822-5681

**Hamann Farms**
Route 3, Box 246
Mason, WI 54856
(715) 765-4654

**Whitetail Institute of
North America**
Route 1, Box 3006
Pintlala, AL 36043
(800) 688-3030
www.deernutrition.com

**Wildlife Nurseries, Inc.**
P.O. Box 2724
Oshkosh, WI 54903

# CHAPTER 9

# DESIGNER FOOD PLOTS
## FOR DEER

There's good reason why alfalfa, the clovers, and other grasses (primarily trefoil, orchard grass, triticale) have long been so popular for agricultural plantings; simply put, they've long proven themselves as superior livestock forages. So it's been a happy coincidence that deer and many other wildlife species have also benefitted from these grasses and legumes.

But the scene is changing. Rapidly growing in popularity in recent years have been the planting of food plots by hunters and sportsmen to meet wildlife's more specific needs. Some of these food types—in particular alfalfa and the clovers—have been either blended or tweaked in other ways to suit a wider range of soil types and climates than their stand-alone counterparts. And they've been bolstered in still other ways to meet the unique nutritional requirements of various wildlife species.

As we saw in the previous chapter, much of this credit must be given to the Whitetail Institute of North America as the first national organization to spearhead a campaign among sportsmen in the nationwide planting of food plots, especially for deer. But WINA has pioneered other innovative plantings, as well.

## THE NO-PLOW PHENOMENON

"When our Imperial Whitetail Clover blend became an overnight success, we began receiving hundreds of requests from deer hunters to develop a high quality seed formulation that could be planted without the use of equipment or cultivation," WINA president Ray Scott explained.

"After six years of study, and the help of thousands of field testers across the country, we developed a product called Imperial No-Plow Wildlife Seed Blend."

By definition, "No-Plow" means that a land manager plants the seed as it is actually done by Mother Nature, on the surface of the ground with minimal or no soil preparation.

This unique, pre-inoculated seed blend is a combination of three types of clover and two types of cereal grains designed to be economical for the hunter to plant in small, odd-shaped, or hard-to-reach areas that have poor soil conditions. This makes No Plow an ideal choice for old logging trails, lowlands that flood every spring but are dry the remainder of the year, dams at remote pond sites, tiny forest clearings, powerline corridors, fence lines, steep hillsides experiencing erosion, and similar locations. Since No-Plow is a "quick-fix" annual legume mixture, it's also the ideal planting option for those who don't own land but have short-term leases and therefore don't want to invest the time and money into a conventional seeding and maintenance of a perennial planting.

In selecting an appropriate site for planting No-Plow, Ray Scott says there are only three requirements to keep in mind. The intended planting site should have fairly good soil moisture, it should have sparse or low-growing vegetation or other ground cover, and it should receive a minimum of four hours of sunlight per day. I've established several No-Plow food plots—each in less than an hour's time and none of them larger than an average living room floor—and the results have been amazing. Deer filtering through deep woodland areas, browsing randomly on this and that, have actually cut new trails into tiny clearings where No-Plow food plots have been established. And where deer rarely came out of dense cover into utility-line corridors and logging trails, or did so only after full dark, we are now more frequently seeing them feeding upon No-Plow even during midday periods.

As a bonus, turkeys, geese, doves, quail, ducks, squirrels, songbirds and many other non-game species are attracted to, and benefit from, No-Plow plantings.

There actually are two No-Plow formulations available from WINA. The first is a spring/summer blend that should be planted in early spring after the last frost. This particular blend provides deer with the extra protein they require during the critical antler-development and fawn-rearing months.

A second fall/winter blend can be planted later in the year when temperatures begin dropping below 55 degrees at night. This particular blend provides deer with additional food sources they'll become tied to during the upcoming, coldest time of year when other food sources are steadily becoming less and less reliable.

In either case, the planting is the same. Simply broadcast-spread the seed by throwing handfuls of the mixture on the ground in random fashion. That's all! In a matter of just a few days, the earliest clover in the blend (called Golden Jumpstart) will be the first to sprout, followed soon by the other components.

As with any food plot effort, it's wise to schedule your planting in accordance with weather forecasts so the seeds will be rained upon within a week.

If this isn't possible, or if a given region has been experiencing a prolonged drought, a healthy

No-Plow is seeded the same as Mother Nature, by broadcast spreading it on the surface.

No-Plow food plot can nevertheless be established, but a garden tiller is required; you'll undoubtedly be able to haul it at least part of the way to the intended planting site by pick-up truck, or in a utility trailer pulled behind an ATV, and can then "walk" it in the remaining distance. In either case, at the planting site, avoid deeply tilling the ground as you would a vegetable garden. All that's necessary is to rough-up the surface to about one-inch deep, broadcast spread your seed mixture, then drag a rake over the ground so the seeds are at least partially covered with soil to protect them from direct sunlight.

If you have any leftover lime from a previous food plot planting, randomly broadcast-spread handfuls of it on your No-Plot area; if not, don't worry because No-Plow is not as pH sensitive as most other plantings. If you have any leftover fertilizer from planting your home vegetable garden, randomly broadcast-spread some of it as well; a standard fertilizer blend of 12-12-12 is just right, but virtually any formulation is better than none at all.

## INTRODUCING BIOLOGIC

More recently, another organization known as BioLogic has become a major player in wildlife management with its own research and testing of seed-blend formulations for the land manager putting in food plots. BioLogic was given birth in 1998 as a subsidiary of the famous Mossy Oak Company that provides sportsmen with premium camouflage clothing and other products.

Dr. Grant Woods, one of the country's foremost research biologists and a storehouse of information pertaining to deer nutrition, reminds land managers that in the wild, very few species of native plants have more than 10 percent protein.

"Yet for whitetails to enjoy optimum health, and for bucks to achieve their antler potential, they must have a diet that provides more than 16 percent crude protein," Woods explains. "BioLogic blends average over 30 percent protein, with some actually reaching 38 percent when the soil medium is prepared properly. Moreover, the high level of palatability of the food plot components, and total digestible nutrients that exceed 80 percent, make BioLogic seed blends a wise choice among the most serious land managers."

It was New Zealand-based Wrightson Nutrition that originally developed the specific seed-types that, in different ratios, comprise BioLogic's various blends.

"The reason New Zealand research has played an important role in our seed-blend formulations has to do with something most sportsmen/landowners in this country are not aware of," explains Toxey Haas, the President of parent company Mossy Oak.

You see, New Zealand is the world's foremost producer of commercially-raised venison for the

NORTHCOUNTRY WHITETAILS

**BioLogic seed blends, widely popular with land managers putting in food plots, is a subsidiary of the famous Mossy Oak Company. The product line has its roots in New Zealand's commercial deer-ranching industry.**

Many land managers think of food plots only in terms of fall hunting seasons. But BioLogic's seed-blends are seasonally-oriented to benefit deer year-around, so does are able to birth and raise healthy fawns and bucks are able to begin laying down heavy antler growth.

restaurant trade and velvet antlers for the pharmaceutical and food-supplement industries. As a result, Wrightson Nutrition has long assisted the country's ranchers in forage plantings designed to rapidly put weight on the animals, improve their health and increase their antler growth.

"In this country, ranchers typically plant what's best for cattle, and so land managers wanting to improve their deer herds have done pretty much the same," Toxey Haas says. "But deer and cattle are different, particularly in their mineral needs and the way they digest plantlife. Just one example is that cattle don't shed their horns and so they don't require large amounts of calcium in their diet for regrowth. Of course, deer eat cattle forage because, other than wild foods, that's what's most commonly made available to them by the livestock growers, but that doesn't mean it's what's best for them."

Consequently, along with the New Zealand deer ranchers, BioLogic has also teamed with Wrightson Nutrition to produce food plot blends specifically targeting whitetails. Equally important, the seed blends grow well in the many varied climate zones and soil conditions where most of North America's deer live.

In looking at Biologic's primary seed blends, which are seasonally-oriented in their components, Grant Woods cautions the land manager.

"Many who are sportsmen tend to want food plots that will be highly attractive to deer during the fall and winter hunting seasons," Woods says. "This is understandable, but it shouldn't be done to the exclusion of additional food plot plantings for the other seasons as well. Sound wildlife management principles call for a nutritional program that spans the entire year."

As a result, if does are in good health in the spring and early summer, they're able to birth healthy fawns and provide sufficient, high-quality milk for them. And if bucks are in good health in the spring and early summer, they're able to meet their body's basic maintenance needs and have enough left over to put into impressive antler growth."

A side benefit to meeting the nutritional needs of your deer and other wildlife is that you'll keep them on your property year-around. Otherwise, if high quality food is absent for many months at a time, they'll drift away

**BioLogic's New Zealand Full Draw is said to draw deer from miles away. It contains six varieties of plantlife, one of which is a foundation wheat bred at Texas A & M University.**

onto other properties and, in so doing, a good percentage of them will become victims of illegal hunting activities or come out second-best in highway skirmishes.

As with all food plot projects discussed in this book, however, keep in mind the axiom we've many times emphasized: No matter what particular planting may be under consideration, a soil-test analysis to determine lime and fertilizer needs will be the foundation upon which the success of that planting rests.

However, in filling out your soil-test application forms, in the space where you indicate the crop you intend to plant, it's not likely the lab analyzing the soil will recognize company brand names or various product descriptions such as No-Plow or BioLogic New Zealand Full Draw.

So simply write in a general plantlife description that as closely as possible represents the components in the product blend you intend to use, such as "clover blend," "sorghum," or "small grain;" to aid in giving the testing university as much information as possible, each bag of seed product is required by law to carry a label describing the cultivar(s) and their percentage of composition.

That said, let's look more closely at BioLogic's unique seed blends.

## BIOLOGIC NEW ZEALAND FULL DRAW

This particular blend is BioLogic's overall best choice. It's the most attractive fall planting because it instantly offers deer a high level of nutrition right from the beginning of germination and continues to do so until the plants mature well after the hunting season. The company promotes its product by saying, "It draws deer for miles, so if you aren't planting Full Draw you better hope your neighbor isn't."

There are six types of annual plantlife in Full Draw, one of which is a strain of foundation-variety wheat bred at Texas A & M University that unlike other grains yields impressive forage tonnage but without any consideration given by the plant to seed-head production.

Another component of Full Draw is four different types of brassica, a broad category of plantlife that matures at different stages and includes rape, turnip, spinach, and mustard varieties. This large-leaf forage grows to a height of 24 inches, is extremely cold-hardy and drought-resistant, and emits a distinct cabbage-like odor that attracts deer from afar. But of special note there's also a variety of white clover in Full Draw that is an annual. As a result, it has a very shallow root mass and thin stem because it channels all of its growth energy into large, highly palatable

NORTHCOUNTRY WHITETAILS

**Another component of New Zealand Full Draw is brassica, a plantlife category that includes rape, turnip, spinach, and mustard varieties that are both cold-hardy and drought-resistant.**

leaves which deer don't just nibble upon; they eat this clover right down to the ground.

Since Full Draw is an annual, it must be reseeded every year.

## BIOLOGIC PREMIUM PERENNIAL BLEND

This particular blend is designed to allow bucks to maximize their antler development. It's also designed to help bucks and does alike to realize their weight-gain potential. This makes it especially well-suited to specific regions where prime natural forage is extremely limited and yet deer living there need quality forage just prior to entering the winter stress period; it's also designed to grow well in a wide variety of soil conditions.

The blend basically consists of three brassicas, two clovers, and a New Zealand chicory that provide highly-digestible protein forage during the spring and summer when antler-growth and fawn development are underway. Because of this growth-surge early in the year, BioLogic researchers recommend over-seeding this particular planting with Fall Attractant sometime in mid- to late-August. I've found the best method is to very lightly disk the food plot, so the existing plantlife/root-structure is not damaged, and then go over the ground a second time with the seed spreader so the seeds will fall into the disk slices. Do this just prior to expected rain and the seeds will quickly germinate. Because this blend is a perennial, expect three to five years of regenerative growth (with supplemental lime and fertilizer, if needed).

## BIOLOGIC SUMMER MANAGEMENT BLEND

Mossy Oak refers to this particular seed blend as "the best health insurance you can provide for your deer herd." It's specifically tailored to the warm-weather growing period in which most plantlife species achieve their highest protein and digestibility levels and thus give deer a more nutritious food intake than natural food alone is able to provide.

Two of the cultivars in the blend are mairaki and manaroa which are the first to appear; the mairaki is a heavy-tonnage producer of highly palatable forage and the manaroa is able to exhibit quick regrowth after heavy grazing. Also in the blend is a sorghum and sudangrass hybrid known as BMR that was developed at Purdue University and is extremely drought-resistant. Additionally, there are bioroa and winfred cultivars in the blend; the bioroa is drought-resistant and the winfred is insect-resistant. Finally, a very tough cultivar known as oamaru within the blend begins coming up in late summer. As a result of this unique combination of plantlife varieties, Summer Management Blend is able to germinate, continue to grow, and withstand cold temperatures, at both ends of the summer growing season.

## BIOLOGIC BIO-MASS

By description, a "bio-mass" is a sudden surge in large quantities of a given high-protein, high-energy form of plantlife that dominates a given unit of environmental area.

BioLogic's Bio-Mass accomplishes this during the spring but especially the summer months when a buck's body metabolism is continually drained of protein, calcium and other nutrients needed to foster skeletal development and antler growth. And it does so by providing bulk quantities of green vegetative matter during a time frame in which less-than-ideal natural habitat is often over-browsed and over-grazed, followed by yielding a grain-carbo-hydrate (soybeans) in the winter. This results in a so-called split-crop in which the maturity of one component of the planting is followed by the upsurge of another to take its place. Bio-Mass is an annual that must be reseeded every year.

BioLogic's Bio-Mass is a lush profusion of plantlife that dominates a food plot in summer when deer are most in need of bulk quantities of high-protein, high-calcium vegetation for skeletal development and antler growth.

## BIOLOGIC NEW ZEALAND FALL ATTRACTANT

This is a highly-palatable blend of forages intended to attract deer to a specific site and thus tighten the animals' core areas of activity.

The plant varieties in this blend result in a greater quantity of forage-mass than Full Draw, but not as much as Bio-Mass, yet are designed to finalize deer antler growth and body weight to each animal's maximum potential for that year just prior to the arrival of most states' cold-weather hunting seasons.

This is accomplished with plant varieties, in particular New Zealand brassicas, that mature at different rates over a time span of eight to twelve weeks. Moreover, the plant varieties are especially well-suited to a wide variety of soil types and even into winter, with snow covering the ground, deer commonly paw down through the white stuff to munch upon the still-green plant remnants.

## BIOLOGIC CLOVER PLUS

Clover Plus is a blend of New Zealand red and white clovers, both of which have leaves much larger than most other clover strains. Therefore, BioLogic researchers contend that, on a per-acre basis, Clover Plus yields far more "bio-mass" than other clover blends and, in so doing, offer deer a forage that's much higher in nutritional intake. As a result, unlike many other clover blends or grass forages that must periodically be mowed, deer keep Clover Plus chewed close to the ground.

The unique aspect of Clover Plus is that it consists of a white clover variety that comes on strong early and late in the season when the weather generally is cool.

But it also has a red clover variety that comes on strong in the summer when the temperature significantly rises. However, as soon as July, August and September temperatures become too hot, even this red clover will begin to wilt and this is when the "Plus" component of the product description kicks in.

The "Plus" component is a variety of chicory that grows to 15 inches tall, has a long tap root similar to a carrot, and delivers the highest known levels of protein and mineral content of all perennial forage crops. But its special attribute is that it thrives in the type of hot summer-weather conditions that commonly stress other food plot plantings. It's not unusual for deer to eat chicory down to ground level, and even paw at the roots, but not to worry; as soon as the temperature begins dropping in early fall and rainfall increases, the white clover comes back. Then when bitter cold weather dormants the clover, the chicory, which is very cold-resistant, comes back still again; some biologists contend the first hard frost triggers sugar production in chicory, causing deer to home-in upon it late in the season.

Clover Plus is a perennial that regenerates for three to five years and BioLogic researchers claim it's the overall tenderest blend currently known.

## PLANTING THE BIOLOGIC BLENDS

The accepted method of seeding all of the BioLogic blends is rather standardized and nearly identical to that of seeding clovers and grasses discussed in Chapters 7 and 8.

First, it's wise to spray a non-selective herbicide over the intended food plot area to kill all existing vegetation. Otherwise, even when the soil is disked to a bare seedbed, billions of weed seeds that have been turned under will quickly germinate and take over the food plot. Then disk the ground in three stages; once in early August, again in late August, and still again in mid-September.

"Next," biologist Grant Woods advises, "spread the seed on the ground a day or two before an anticipated steady rain. In this manner, the seed falls into the disk slices and then, shortly after the rainfall moistens the ground, the seed quickly germinates before a crust has been allowed to form on the soil surface. Otherwise, if you plant too far ahead of a rain, the seeds don't have the required soil moisture to germinate. And if you plant shortly after a rain when the ground is wet, the ground will begin to dry before the seeds can germinate and a large percentage of them will not be able to push up through the hardened surface layer of soil. Within two weeks after emergence of the seeds, then top dress with fertilizer. Generally, an application of about 100 pounds of 13-13-13 or triple-12 per acre is what a soil-test analysis will call for."

The one exception to all of this is BioLogic's Summer Management

BioLogic's Clover Plus is a unique blend of red and white clovers that, unlike other clover blends, don't have to be regularly mowed because deer keep it chewed down close to the ground. There's also a variety of chicory in the blend; when deer eat it down, there's an upsurge in the white clover, and when cold weather dormants the clover, the chicory comes back yet again.

The most effective planting of Premium Perennial Blend is early in the year but then in mid-August it should be lightly disked and over-seeded with BioLogic's Fall Attractant which serves to tighten the local deer herd's core-activity areas.

Blend, in which disking is not recommended just prior to seeding because it will see the seeds buried too deeply. Better is to prepare a smooth seedbed, broadcast the seed, and then simply go over it with a cultipacker or roller to barely press the seeds into the surface of the soil.

Incidentally, we mentioned earlier the wise practice of strip-cropping the larger food plots. That is, planting two or more forages side by side so that about the time one forage has peaked in maturity, and is beginning to go downhill, another is just beginning to come on strong. In this manner, several different strip-cropped food plots in different regions of the property can literally hold the deer population on that acreage indefinitely.

More specifically, with BioLogic products, the recommended advice, whenever possible, is to plant an appropriate clover blend around the outer perimeter of the food plot with a Bio-Mass planting in the middle.

Finally, BioLogic also produces a vitamin-mineral supplement for deer, as well as seed blends for quail, turkeys, doves, ducks and geese. These subjects are discussed in later chapters.

## SEED SOURCES

**BioLogic**
P.O. Box 757
West Point, MS 39773
(601) 494-8859
www.mossyoak.com

**Whitetail Institute of North America**
239 Whitetail Trail
Pintlala, AL 36043
(800) 688-3030
www.deernutrition.com

# CHAPTER 10

## SPECIALTY
# DEER FOODS

Increasingly, wildlife managers who own or lease land are planting food plot forages that simply weren't available as recently as only ten years ago. As we've seen in previous chapters, they're planting the new high-tech clover blends now on the market, as well as other combination-plantings of legumes, grasses and broadleaf plants. And they're seeing an explosion in deer populations, with bucks commonly sporting larger antlers than previously known in their regions. In so doing, they're simultaneously enhancing the health, well-being and growing numbers of other game and non-game populations such as turkeys, upland gamebirds and a host of songbird species.

Of course, the clovers and designer forages described earlier are primarily soft, vegetation-type foods that do best during the mild- and warm-weather months. Conversely, the forages to be discussed here, although a few specialty grasses are included, are mostly beans, peas, small cereal grains (wheat, oats, barely, rye) and larger grains (primarily corn and soybeans). Many of these bridge the gap by doing well during the cool- and cold-weather months. And some, such as corn and soybeans in particular, provide forage throughout the coldest winter months; they're no longer growing, of course, but their rigid stalks hold the ears and bean pods above the snow level. Moreover, many of these deer forages can be planted as stand-alone foods, particularly in the case of corn and soybeans, while many of the others are commonly planted in combination with others.

## WILD WORLD OF SEED BLENDS

Noted biologist Larry Weishuhn, who has established wildlife management programs for numerous ranchers and landowners across North America, has a good deal of insight when it comes to food plots for whitetails. Recently he teamed-up with Texas Seed Company to offer seed selections he particularly likes for deer food plots, but there also are several other leading companies in wildlife seed production; see the listing at the end of this chapter.

Most of these seed companies now make available to land managers an enormous variety of seed-types that can be planted as stand-alone food plots. But increasingly, they're also becoming well known for custommixing any combination of these seeds to the landowner's specifications.

Among wildlife managers targeting whitetails in particular but also wanting to benefit other game and non-game species, the most popular varieties for spring and summer mixes and stand-alone plantings include the following: red ripper peas, Mr. Whitetail peas, Chinese red peas, alfalfa, ryegrass, mung beans, browntop millet, sunflowers, corn, iron & clay peas, combine cowpeas, partridge peas, summer peas, hegari, lab-lab, hybrid pearl millet, German foxtail millet, spring wheat, grain sorghum, WGF sorghum, Illinois bundleflower, and spring oats.

The most popular varieties for fall and winter mixes and stand-alone plantings include: browntop millet, hybrid pearl millet, sesame, winter wheat, hegari, sunflowers, WGF sorghum, Austrian winter peas, triticale, rye, barley, and winter oats.

**Part of every food plot program for deer should include stand-alone crops such as small and large grains. These bridge the gap between the high-protein spring/summer growth needs of wildlife and their high-carbohydrate fall/winter energy needs.**

But which should you consider?

"For deer, specifically, I always recommend hunters and landowners establish two types of food plots," Larry told me. "One should consist of those in the winter-foods category to help the animals through a period of great physiological stress. My personal favorites to plant in these plots include winter oats,

With only minor variations, food plots for stand-alone crops are prepared in basically the same manner. First, the soil is tilled to medium depth and then fertilizer disked in.

winter wheat, triticale, or Austrian winter peas."

"Late spring and early summer food plots also are necessary," Weishuhn continues, "because during this period deer likewise are subjected to high nutritional needs. Does must give birth to healthy twins, nurse them, and then wean them onto the most nutritional foods available locally. Meanwhile, bucks are experiencing the critical developmental stages of antler growth. In these food plots, I recommend hunters plant WGF sorghum, hegari, alfalfa, soybeans, or summer cowpeas."

"Whether planted as stand-alone food plots, or as blends, these are all high-protein forages that require only minimal land preparation such as disking, followed by broadcasting the seed to shallow-sew it and then cultipacking the soil or going over it with a roller," Weishuhn says. "Any additional instructions that may apply to a specific seed variety or formulation are included with the shipment."

On larger-size food plots it's wise to also strip-crop with different seed varieties that have different maturity dates. Or, if it's a stand-alone variety, at least stagger your plantings by several weeks so that when one segment has matured and most of it has been eaten down, another is just beginning to reach its prime.

It's also a common practice to blend any of the cereal grains with a legume such as clover or alfalfa. The reason is because, as with all blends, deer like variety. But more specifically, cereal grains require high levels of soil nitrogen to do well and can quickly deplete the soil of this element; since legumes extract nitrogen from the air and fix it to their root nodules, they are continually replenishing the element.

Of course, once a landowner's seed choices have been made, the next step prior to planting should be having a soil sample analyzed to determine lime and fertilizer needs.

A soil-test analysis is particularly important in the case of beans and peas, since all of these varieties are legumes that do best in a soil pH of at least 6.7 or higher and therefore almost always require a lime application several months before planting time.

In planting all peas and beans, remember that they're legumes that require periodic lime applications to retain a high soil pH level.

Two other notes of worth. Since there are sub-varieties of many of the above seed choices, it's important when placing an order with any seed company to describe the geographic region where you live in terms of latitude and predominant soil type; in so doing, the company will tailor your seed order to your particular climate and average annual rainfall.

Also, in the case of those seed varieties that must be inoculated prior to planting, it's a wise and time-saving practice to pay a small additional amount to have the seeds pre-inoculated prior to shipping. Some of the distributors, such as Texas Seed Company, also ship their seeds pre-treated with Germax, one of the Trophy Xcellerator's family of growth stimulants designed to promote rapid germination, growth and high yield.

## CORN & SOYBEANS

Corn and soybeans are widely popular with deer and food plot managers alike. But you needn't purchase these planting forages from distant companies and then have to additionally pay hefty postage charges to have 40-pound bags of the seed shipped to you. Corn and soybeans are both sure to be available at your local farm supply store. Moreover, they'll have the particular varieties that have proven track records of doing well in your specific geographic region.

As emphasized many times before, just be sure to do a little sleuthing to make sure corn and soybeans aren't being planted in large quantities on neighboring farmlands.

Corn and soybeans are superior deer forages because of their high-carbohydrate, high-energy content. However, if financial concerns play a major role in your food plot choices, you'll get far more bang for your buck if you focus primarily upon high-protein foods such as the clovers and other grass blends.

There are several ways to plant corn and soybeans, but in all cases a soil test analysis comes first.

Following the application of the required lime, those involved in full-time farming operations, who always strive for maximum per-acre yields, then make use of assorted types of planters to simultaneously sew the seeds and apply fertilizer. This is then followed, in weeks to come, by cultivating between the plant rows to reduce competing weed-growth, or by applying an appropriate selective herbicide. And this, in turn, is often followed in weeks to come by side-dressing with fertilizer.

But putting in a corn or soybean food plot for deer need not be as involved. The only critical concerns are lime and fertilizer applications and preparing an adequate seedbed by first deep-plowing, or chisel-plowing, and then smoothing the soil with a disk or combination harrow-disk. Moreover, mechanized planting equipment isn't absolutely required for merely establishing a corn or soybean food plot because there shouldn't be any follow-up need to cultivate between the plant rows, apply herbicides, or even side-dress with additional fertilizer to achieve at least a modest per-acre yield; nor will there be any future need to efficiently maneuver harvesting equipment down uniformly spaced rows of the grainfields.

However, every land manager's situation is unique and thus provides him with numerous options.

One possibility is having a neighbor farmer plant the corn or beans for you. Let's say he would like to plant corn or beans on his own land but all of his acreage presently is committed to other crops. In this case, he may be glad to enter into an agreement to plant one or more of your food plots on a "shares" basis; in this situation, he provides the equipment, seed, fertilizer, and labor and takes 75 percent of the crop at harvest time. You, in turn, receive the remaining 25 percent of the crop but you tell him to leave it standing for wildlife forage. Just be sure the farmer does the harvesting in such a manner that your share is not in the form of one or two long rows in the middle of the field; to ensure daylight visitation by deer, the remaining crop should ideally be in the form of a block or rectangle that's situated adjacent to the heaviest cover in the immediate area.

Another option, if a neighbor farmer doesn't need corn or soybeans, is to simply pay him a fee to custom plant your ground. In this case, the customary arrangement is for the landowner to provide the seed and fertilizer and then additionally pay the farmer $25 per hour to prepare the ground and plant the crop, using his machinery.

To row crop, it's necessary to use a one-row planter pulled behind an ATV or a multiple-row planter pulled behind a small tractor.

The final option is to plant the corn or beans yourself, and it's possible to do this with an ATV and several pieces of downsized, pull-behind equipment; you won't likely achieve the same high per-acre yield as if a full-time farmer had put in the crop, but it should be more than sufficient to serve as forage for the local deer and wildlife.

For do-it-yourselfers, a few general tips are in order. When buying the seed, keep in mind our earlier recommendation that strip-cropping provides a longer-term food source than single-cropping. So after having a soil-test sample analyzed and acquiring whatever lime and fertilizer is needed, ask your seed dealer about early- and late-maturing corn or bean varieties that may be available. If only one type is recommended for your particular geographic region, stagger your plantings in two or three week intervals so that different blocks or rows are always in different growth stages.

With corn, also keep in mind that it's necessary to plant in blocks of no less than eight rows. To successfully bear a maximum number of ears, a corn planting must be able to cross-pollinate; therefore, for example, eight relatively short rows in a square block will produce a much higher yield than an equal number of plants in only two rows that are four times as long.

With both corn and beans, also keep in mind the same advice we earlier gave regarding all seed plantings: They should be sewed at a depth that is approximately four times their seed length. Consequently, while clover seeds, many of which are no larger than a pinhead, are generally planted less than 1/4-inch deep, or in some cases are barely pressed into the surface of the soil, most corn varieties need to be covered with at least two inches of soil. The recommended planting depth for soybeans is 1-1/2 inches.

Dozens of corn cultivars have been developed and many do best in certain climates or soil conditions. Your local seed store can tell you which variety is the most popular in your region.

In any forage planting, soil moisture is a critical component in required planting depth; so if the ground is very dry, increase the planting depth by 25 percent.

Those on the tightest budgets can nevertheless put in corn and soybean food plots (ideally, no larger than one-half acre in size) by using a garden tiller to break the ground. Then broadcast the seed, randomly throwing only small handfuls at a time in an attempt to acquire an individual spacing of at least 10 inches between corn seeds and 6 inches between soybean seeds so they won't be overly crowded and forced to compete for available sunlight, ground moisture and soil nutrients. Then either hand-rake the ground or pull behind an ATV a weighted square of chain-link fence to cover the seeds with soil.

Interestingly, deer often "target" soybeans to the exclusion of other available feeding opportunities. Therefore, many land managers who have

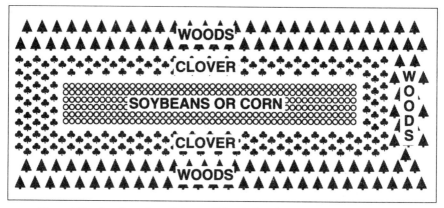

To avoid having deer devastate small food plots in corn or soybeans, many land managers use the planting method called "fencing." This causes deer, when they first exit cover, to pause and begin filling-up on the regenerative salad before they reach the steak.

only small food plots, less than an acre in size, like to plant soybeans, but also sometimes corn, right in the middle of the plot, surrounded on all sides by a grass forage such as clover or alfalfa.

This planting procedure is called "fencing" and it has the effect of "stopping" deer as they leave adjacent woodland cover and encouraging them to begin eating the grass forage first and at least partially filling their paunches so they don't as quickly reach and begin devastating the soybean or corn planting, thus allowing the beans or corn to last over a longer period of time.

## SHRUBS, VINES & BERRIES

In line with the land-manager's philosophy of providing deer and other wildlife with a wide variety of foraging opportunities, consider shrubs, vines and berries. When spring planting of certain forages in conventional food plots is done, and fall planting of still other food plots is still many weeks away, the in-between months are a splendid time to engage in other plantings in still other places.

Japanese honeysuckle is high on a deer's hit list but also favored by turkeys, quail and ruffed grouse. This is a perennial, woody, vining ground cover that grows to six feet tall and provides excellent cover. But also, it is one of the very few plant species that remains green and palatable throughout winter months and can reach a protein level as high as 20 percent.

Honeysuckle can become an intrusive plant species that spreads and quickly overtakes other native plants, so if it's already evident on your property, don't plant it. Moreover, if it's already evident but barely surviving, you can jump-start it by fertilizing it; should it eventually start to get out of control, you can knock it back a bit with a non-selective herbicide.

Honeysuckle does well in areas that are partially shaded, such as steep north-facing hillsides. It also thrives in rugged draws, stream bottoms and drainages with rock-strewn ground, along the leading edges of back roads and interior woodland trails, and along fencerows and field edges.

State wildlife departments commonly sell honeysuckle as seedlings in flats containing 24 plants each, or they can provide a list of nurseries or seed dealers that carry honeysuckle. Seedlings should be planted with a five-foot spacing, using a common garden trowel.

After spring planting is finished, it's time to fertilize native plantlife. Deer and numerous other wildlife forage heavily upon Japanese honeysuckle and blackberries, in particular, and their yield can be boosted with an annual application of 36-3-7.

Existing honeysuckle plants should be fertilized twice a year, once in early spring and again 60 days later. Most agronomists recommend Scott's Native Plant Fertilizer (36-3-7) or any similar formulation at the recommended bag rate; with newly planted seedlings, wait one year for the plants to become established before fertilizing.

Native berry plants (blackberry, raspberry, elderberry) are eagerly foraged upon by deer, gamebirds and songbirds. They do especially well on higher ground, particularly open, sun-drenched hillsides and along fencerows and field edges. Deer forage upon the green leaves and buds in spring, eat the berries throughout the summer, then browse upon the "canes" in winter.

Domesticated berry plants are available from nurseries but they're expensive. So most landowners simply search for existing, native stands, and then improve them with a fertilizer application of 10-10-10 in early spring.

If berry bushes are evident on a property, but scant in number, landowners

Most state wildlife departments offer free wildlife seed blends to landowners. They contain a wide variety of annual grasses, large grains and cereals tailored to each state's climate. They're well-suited to the smallest food plots when you haven't yet decided upon a perennial planting.

have relatively good success in digging up individual canes in winter, transplanting them elsewhere and, if they successfully take root and leaf-out the following spring, giving them an immediate fertilizer application.

There are still other plant varieties worth considering that will favor deer and other wildlife populations in those areas of a property not planted to food plots. Check with your state wildlife office for plant recommendations that are indigenous to your particular region but are not currently evident on your own property.

But heed one caveat: Avoid at all costs the planting of kudzu, multiflora rose, and autumn olive; at first, they provide deer and gamebirds with excellent cover and foraging opportunities but they're all highly invasive and can literally take over, spread widely and choke out large tracts of acreage.

## FREE WILDLIFE SEED BLENDS

Because establishing food plots has proven so beneficial to deer and other wildlife species, many state game departments are now offering so-called wildlife seed packets to the public. These two-pound seed packets are usually free, the only requirement being that you must own or lease a minimum of five acres of land.

The contents of these packets may vary between states in accordance

**Wildlife seed blends attract not only deer but also turkeys, waterfowl and gamebirds that forage upon the cornucopia of grains throughout the winter.**

with regional climatic and soil conditions but in all cases they contain a wide assortment of wildlife forages. The most recent packets I've obtained (in Ohio) contained seeds which later resulted in very diverse food plots containing sunflowers, millet, corn, orchard grass, rye, soybeans, birdsfoot trefoil, red clover, oats, blackberries, and several other seed-producing varieties I couldn't identify but undoubtedly were selected for specific songbird species.

I wouldn't use a prime food plot area for one of these plantings. However, virtually every parcel of land has numerous, small, out-of-the-way places where nothing of wildlife value is growing and perhaps where the terrain is too steep or rugged to allow the use of mechanized equipment. This was exactly the case with regards to our earlier mention of No-Plow seed blend in Chapter 9, but it applies equally well to state wildlife seed packets.

To plant, simply rough-up the ground with a garden rake, randomly broadcast the seeds, cover lightly with soil, then throw on several handfuls of generic all-purpose fertilizer such as triple-12.

## SPECIALTY SEED SOURCES

**Adams-Briscoe Seed Company**
P.O. Box 19
Jackson, GA 30233
(770) 775-7826
abseed@juno.com

**Pennington Seeds**
Box 290
Madison, GA 30650
(800) 285-7333
www.penningtonseed.com

**Buck Forage Oats**
P.O. Box 43
Stuttgart, AR 72160
(800) 299-6287
www.buckforage.com

**Tecomate Seed Company**
Rt. 2, Box 77A
San Juan, TX 78589
(800) 332-4054

**Texas Seed Company**
P.O. Drawer 599
Kenedy, TX 78119
(800) 321-5673

# CHAPTER 11

## SUPPLEMENTAL
# DEER FEEDING

Supplementally feeding deer is controversial because of the fear that it can foster dependency.

That's entirely possible, but in my opinion only if it's done in unique, highly controlled situations (such as high-fenced acreage) and to the exclusion of putting in food plots and enhancing native plant growth on the property.

As a result, I prefer to see landowners using sound, balanced wildlife management principles and for supplemental feeding to be only part of an overall larger plan.

In some instances the practice may even be

Supplemental feeding, although controversial, is a small part of an overall management plan that enhances the health of bucks and does alike.

looked upon as a first-aid kit to periodically be brought out to enable deer to survive when times are tough. Particularly in the northernmost states, winters can be brutal. Then there are the arid regions of the country where growing anything but cactus can be an exercise in futility. Elsewhere, extreme drought or

In harsh conditions, especially during droughts or brutally cold winters, offering deer more food than what nature alone can provide can literally save their lives.

flooding can periodically wipe out deer habitat and take any previously existing forage with it.

In any of these worst-case scenarios, supplementally feeding deer can literally save their lives. But even in situations that are not so severe, supplemental feeding can be "that little something extra" that prevents the animals from some years experiencing a nutritional downhill slide that impairs fawn development, antler growth and the overall health of the herd.

There may even be situations in which the weather is normal during a given year but a land manager, for whatever reason, has not yet had the opportunity to put in food plots or enhance native plant growth but nevertheless wants to immediately get started doing something—anything—to improve the quality of his wildlife populations.

## INEXPENSIVE FEEDING PROGRAMS

In a previous chapter we mentioned the importance of periodically mowing food plots planted to clovers and other perennial grasses to reduce weed competition. And we said that if a land manager doesn't have his own mowing equipment, he can have the work done on a "shares basis" with a neighbor farmer who cuts the forage and receives three-quarters of the resulting bales for his own livestock usage.

The remaining quarter share, which can easily amount to dozens of bales, goes to the landowner to use as he sees fit. This highly nutritious forage, particularly alfalfa, can be put under protective cover and then later, during prolonged periods of severe weather, hauled to random locations and scattered on the ground.

In the scientific community, there is evidence that too much supplemental feeding of deer, or a heavy emphasis upon just one type of forage—hay or otherwise—can disrupt the digestive systems of the animals and cause more harm than good. Studies have shown that starving deer don't have the microfauna to digest roughage in their rumens. It seems the key, therefore, is to not allow the deer on one's property to reach the starving point in the first place. So it's wise to ration one's hay bales over a period of time, scatter them in widely separated locations on the property, and supplement them with other food offerings.

Similarly, when future food plots are in the planning stages, keep in mind biologist Larry Weishuhn's admonition that at least half of their total allocated acreage should be put into winter foods such as winter oats, winter peas, or stiff-stalk forages that remain available even when there is snowcover, such as soybeans and corn.

In northern states, a percentage of food plots should go into stiff-stalk winter forages, particularly grains. Here, a mix of corn and sorghum planted primarily for deer has been lightly disked to also make it available to turkeys, gamebirds, small game and songbirds.

Meanwhile, a method of habitat enhancement that will provide deer with an excellent food source is a warm-season project that can be undertaken purely at one's convenience. This is herbiciding areas of hardwood brush along the edges of the property's interior roads, woodland trails and field edges. The recommended herbicide for this type of work is Arsenal and it can be applied with a common backpack sprayer that holds three gallons and has an application wand. Be sure to follow the labeling instructions.

The best time to herbicide these brushy areas is from late spring to early summer. When the brown-out occurs within the next week or so, indicating the junkwood ground-cover has been killed, throw random handfuls of all-purpose fertilizer (such as triple-13) on the treated areas.

In no time at all, lush plantlife that previously was dormant due to over-crowding and overshading will spring to life. Of course, later that year, the green leaves will quickly succumb to the cold temperatures. But remaining will be countless, tender, new-growth shoots and stems and even start-up tree seedlings that deer will eagerly browse upon throughout the winter.

The following spring/summer, herbicide a similar area on another part of the property, and so on, as part of an annual, rotating program of winter native-food production.

Most who own or lease land use spare time in the spring and summer to also cut firewood. When you do so, don't lop off trees flush with the ground. Leave an approximate 18-inch stump and "score" the top of it with cuts to collect rainwater. In little time the "mother" stump, in an attempt to propagate herself, will foster countless sucker shoots that will produce tender buds and branchtips that deer will eagerly browse upon later that winter and in subsequent years.

## USING FEED BINS AND TROUGHS

The purpose of feed bins and troughs is to keep food dry for longer periods of time than occurs when it's simply dumped on the ground.

Bins and troughs can be constructed at little cost from scrap lumber. But you have to invest your time, and lumber exposed to weather will rot in just a few short years. I've always preferred buying used commercial bins and troughs at small farm auctions. They're made of durable sheet metal, come in a wide variety of shapes and sizes, and often can be had for just a few bucks apiece.

## MECHANICAL FEEDERS

Presently on the market are a wide variety of prefabricated, sheetmetal wildlife feeders in square or drum shape. They range in feed-holding capacity from 5-gallon "bucket size" models to enormous models holding 2,000 pounds of feed; the most popular are those that hold 100 to 300 pounds.

Most feeders are of the free-standing variety and are mounted on upright stilts, some quite high above the ground, but others squat on low legs. Other variations don't use legs of any type but are designed to be hung via a short length of chain from a stout, overhead tree limb.

The advantage of the smaller mechanical feeders is their inexpensive cost; the great disadvantage is that in some instances they can require re-filling every few days. Conversely, the larger-capacity models are more expensive but require refilling as infrequently as only once a month.

Moreover, feeders on low legs, close to the ground, can easily be tampered with and damaged by raccoons and bears, while those high off the ground are some-what out of harm's way.

Another important matter that should influence a buyer's decision is " how" the feeder is filled. It sounds simple enough to merely remove the top lid and dump in bags of feed. But if the feeder is on stilts and its top lid is therefore 10 feet off the ground, and you've situated the feeder in rugged terrain not easily accessible by vehicle, sud-denly your life has become a lot more complicated!

Some manufacturers have remedied the problem of fill-

Assorted feed bins and troughs, purchased at farm auctions, can be used for woodland feeding programs.

ing their feeders by making use of a hand-crank winch, of the type commonly used on boat trailers, to raise and lower the feeder, no matter whether it's on stilts or hung from an overhead tree branch.

The concept works fine but the winch, its braided wire cable, its tripod- or tree-mounting bracket, and its overhead pulley assembly, adds significantly to the overall cost of each feeder.

Every land manager will therefore have to study company brochures, feeder specifications, available accessories, and prices, and then make a decision based upon what best fits his unique needs.

In my own case, I use 100-gallon feeders. Since I have four of them, they only have to be filled every two weeks during the winter season and this is not a great inconvenience because I live year-around on my property. Since I use the type that are elevated on medium-height stilts, their fill-lids are only 8 feet off the ground. In this manner, I can use a four-wheeler to easily haul feed bags to each feeder's location no matter what the weather may be

Mechanical feeders range widely in size. The smallest 5 gallon models are best for remote, rugged terrain; this model is battery operated.

Larger feeders with a 50 gallon capacity sit slightly off the ground. Some models use gravity to intermittently dispense feed and others are battery-operated.

doing; then, I can just as easily stand on the ATV's rear cargo rack to remove the feeder's fill-lid and dump in the bags of feed. It works for me!

When deciding upon a mechanical feeder, an equally important consideration is the manner in which the feeder dispenses feed. Paradoxically, the least expensive to buy are the gravity-fed models, but they're the most expensive to operate because they continuously drop feed upon the ground until the storage hopper is empty. Much better are feeders that are electronically-activated by means of a 6- or 12-volt wet-cell battery; a tiny solar panel gathers sunlight energy during the daylight hours and trickle-charges the battery. Other electronically-activated feeders, usually the smallest-capacity models, may operate with several dry-cell, flashlight-type batteries.

Also worth consideration is the type of timing mechanism that determines "when" each day the feed is dispensed. The least expensive models have a simple photocell that turns the feeder on for brief periods of time at dawn and dusk. But much better are the timing mechanisms that have a small keypad, allowing the feeder to be programmed to dispense feed at many specific times of day; deluxe models can be programmed to dispense feeding "events" as often as 24 times a day.

It's common for those who like to hunt in the vicinity of their feeders to program them to dispense feed during those times when they customarily like to occupy their stands or blinds; when the feeder activates and begins dispensing feed, it's often like ringing a dinner bell, especially if there are no other food sources nearby.

The only hard-and-fast rule about programming a feeder is to not set its timing mechanism to dispense feed after dark because nocturnal creatures—raccoons in particular but also opossums, armadillos, bears, rabbits, hares, javelina and wild hogs—will consume much of the food intended for target species such as deer, turkeys and gamebirds.

The most popular feeders are of 100 gallon capacity and are mounted on stilts to prevent animals from damaging the unit. A spin-disk on the bottom side throws the grain a long distance, and a hand-crank winch lowers the unit for refilling.

Unlike gravity feeders, the electronic models have on the underneath, bottom side some sort of scatter wheel or disk that, when activated, spins and throws grain varying distances around the base of the feeder and in different patterns; some models are even directional.

As might be expected, the programmable-keypad activation systems are the most expensive to purchase, the dawn-and-dusk photocell/wet-battery activation systems the next most expensive, and the dry-cell battery systems are the least expensive to purchase. But other factors may come into play; for example, having to regularly replace dry-cell batteries in many feeders during the course of a long winter can be very costly.

How many feeders does a land manager need? Well, keep in mind that deer commonly exhibit a feeding hierarchy. Consequently, if only one or two feeders are available on a large property, the dominant animals will keep the subordinates away. So the rule of thumb is to have three feeders per every 100 acres of land.

When deciding upon places to situate such feeders, never place them in view of roads where they'll attract not only deer but also the interest of passersby. I prefer to situate them in small clearings near heavy-cover regions to encourage deer to use them during daylight periods and allowing them to do so "privately." However, I also like to have a view of at least one feeder from my kitchen window for no other reason than the simple pleasure of watching wildlife.

## WHAT TYPE OF FOOD?

Shelled corn purchased at a nearby feed mill is commonly used in all types of feeders; be sure to buy only certified field corn that has been analyzed to be free of any toxins or bacteria that commonly infect corn.

Corn is high in carbohydrate-content and is therefore a high-energy food comparable to acorns. But since corn averages only 8 percent digestible protein, and since I usually have at least one food plot in planted corn that

Another variation of feeder mounts on a tree trunk. On the side of the drum, this model has a solar panel that recharges its battery, and a keypad to program specific feeding times. Note the stovepipe on the tree trunk to prevent bears from damaging the unit.

I leave standing, I prefer to fill my feeders with soybeans, which approach 45 percent protein. However, deer are at first reluctant to eat soybeans dispensed from a feeder. So most land managers begin with a 50-50 blend of corn and soybeans and, about one month into the winter, switch to 100-percent beans.

I also like to use the same feed-blend that's fed to hoofed animal species in zoos and wildlife parks. It's relatively inexpensive, put up in 50-pound bags and available under a number of brand names; the most widely known is Sweetena. Such blends typically consist of corn, oats and wheat, but in some cases other grains as well and even vitamin supplements, along with a "binder" of cane syrup or sorghum molasses; the protein content, depending upon the particular blend, approaches 30 percent.

However, a word of caution. A cardinal rule is to never use in a mechanical scatter-type feeder any feed that has a binder. These feeds are intended for use only in open-air, free-choice feeding situations such troughs or bins; in a mechanical feeder, the rather "sticky" consistency of such feeds will gum-up and eventually ruin the feeder's electronic dispensing mechanism. As mentioned earlier, the recommended food for mechanical feeders is always some form of dry grain such as shell corn or soybeans.

Purina Mills, long famous for its animal foods, also caters to wildlife managers with four different Deer Chow blends that vary in grain-mixture and protein content; they're available at feed mills across the country.

Rapidly increasing in popularity are also commercial, pelleted wildlife foods that commonly consist of blends of several grains along with vitamin and mineral supplements. Since these pelleted foods have a porous consistency, they tend to swell up in high-humidity levels and if allowed to become damp they break apart. Therefore, it's not recommended they be used in electronically-activated, sling-type feeders. Even in gravity-fed feeders they can form "globs" that restrict their otherwise free-flowing tendency, so use them only in covered, free-choice feed bins and troughs.

One final note. At the beginning of this chapter we mentioned that some people worry about deer establishing a dependency upon supplemental feeding programs. However, it's been my experience, and that of many other land managers who maintain seasonal food plots, to have a contrary opinion.

We've found that deer which have been supplementally fed to more easily make it through difficult periods of severe winter weather tend to quickly break this bond at the first hints of spring green-up.

In fact, even when a late-spring snowfall unexpectedly blankets the terrain, it's not unusual to see deer avoid the feeders, preferring instead to forage upon tender tree buds that have recently broken-out and even paw down through the white stuff to reach green grasses that have just begun to emerge. Consequently, my last filling of feeders (in Ohio) is usually done in early March; farther north or south, this may vary somewhat.

**Where you situate your feeders is important. Never place them in view of roads. And consider how you'll access them, particularly in bad weather, to refill them.**

# FEEDERS & FEED SOURCES

**Deer Feeder Suppliers**
177 Hopkinsville St.
Cerulean, KY 42215

**Moultrie Feeders**
P.O. Box 20322
Birmingham, AL 35216
(205) 942-0920

**Kenco Game Feeders**
8575 West 110th St.
Overland Park, KS 66210
(913) 317-9600
www.outlandsports.com

**Lehman Feeders**
RR 3, Box 53
Corpus Christi, TX 78415

**Magnum Hunting Products**
1306 FM 1092 Rd.
Missouri City, TX 77459

**MegaBucks**
205 Woodrow Ave.
Sinking Spring, PA 19608
(800) 634-2282

**On-Time Feeders**
Box 631856
Nacodoches, TX 75963

**Outback Feeders**
Route 8, Box 548
Gilmer, TX 75644
(903) 734-4210
www.outbackfeeders.com

**Purina Mills**
1401 S. Hanley Rd.
St. Louis, MO 63144
(800) 227-8941

**RealBark Feeders**
Box 2078
Henderson, TX 75653

**R & S Hunting & Fishing Products**
27618 Natural Bridge Caverns
San Antonio, TX 7812
(800) 584-0498

**Superbowl Deer Feeders**
4858 W.P. Hardy Rd.
LaGrange, NC 28551
(252) 566-9020
www.superbowlfeeders.com

**Sweeney Feeding Systems**
321 Waring-Welfare Rd.
Boerne, TX 78006
(800) 443-4244
www.SweeneyFeeders.com

**Texas Hunter Products**
4242 IH-10 East
San Antonio, TX 78219
(800) 969-3337

# CHAPTER 12

## MINERAL MAGIC FOR
# BIGGER ANTLERS

As we've seen in the previous chapters, hunters who own their own property, lease a tract of real estate, or have a long-standing friendship with a farmer or landowner, are increasingly beginning to intelligently manage the deer roaming that acreage. And they're finding that not only are they able to make dramatic improvements in the quality and health of their deer herds but are now enjoying the taking of bucks with much larger than average racks.

In this chapter there is yet a final thing we can do to greatly benefit any population of deer and that's to provide them with minerals and vitamins.

### TIMING IS THE KEY

Remember the old advice about putting out a salt block for deer and how you tried it and never noticed any increase in the quality of deer in your area? In fact, I'll bet you rarely even saw a big buck in the vicinity of the block. Well, we now have the answers to those dilemmas.

Contrary to popular belief, placing out a salt block doesn't help antler growth. In fact, bucks purposely visit mineral licks only during the spring; visits at other times of year are random, when a deer is coincidentally in the area.

Bucks and does alike utilize mineral licks year-around but only infrequently during the fall/winter hunting seasons; at this time, whenever they happen to randomly be in the vicinity of a salt block or mineral lick, they may briefly pause to sample a bit of its salty flavor. But it's during the spring and early summer when their body metabolisms actually develop a strong craving for minerals, causing bucks and does to repeatedly visit licks every day and each time remain for sometimes extended periods.

It's early in the year when does need additional minerals to give birth to healthy fawns and provide the offspring during their first several days with highly nutritious colostrum (a "that's high in minerals, antibodies and nutrients") and in following weeks with "true" milk. It's also when bucks are just beginning to lay down antler growth and need the calcified building blocks that minerals provide.

Yet, although deer love the taste of salt and will lick and chew at the blocks in the spring, salt alone does almost nothing to enhance their overall body health. They need a special blend of minerals.

Unfortunately, most regions of the country are deficient in one or more trace minerals in the soil and water, and consequently also in the plant matter deer eat and the water they drink. In turn, that shortcoming is reflected in less than optimal deer reproduction and unimpressive antler growth.

A prime example of this was our previous, long-held belief that spike bucks were genetically inferior animals that should be culled. But then I had an experience that entirely changed my mind. It had to do with a friend who owns a game farm where he raises all manner of animals and exotic birds.

One year he acquired a 1-1/2 year old whitetail buck with three-inch spike antlers. Since the fenced enclosure where the deer was kept offered only a marginal amount of grass, my friend supplementally fed the deer cracked corn and alfalfa. He also placed in the pen a mineral block.

Amazingly, during the very next spring/summer period the young buck grew an impressive 8-point rack with an 18-inch spread! In the wild, it would be a shame to see a buck of this genetic potential intentionally culled as a spike when the young deer obviously was only malnourished.

That incident, confirmed since by studies at wildlife experiment stations around the country, have provided convincing evidence that spike bucks are not necessarily genetically inferior animals. Many young bucks with small or disfigured antlers may have simply been given birth by weakened does coming off an unusually harsh winter. Consequently, the newborn fawns were in poor physical condition to begin with, and this was reflected in a first set of very small antlers because their bodies commandeered all of their nutrient intake to first meet basic survival needs and then go into beginning muscle and skeletal growth; in such cases, nature establishes its priorities and decides that antler development can wait until subsequent years when (and if) bodily development achieves normalcy.

In recent years, wildlife biologists have also come to another revelation pertaining to bucks. The sad truth is that bucks that manage to elude hunters many still not survive from one hunting season to the next, especially those bucks which are approaching maturity and are the most energetic breeders.

OHIO DIVISION OF WILDLIFE

**Antler growth hinges upon trace minerals in the soil which are absorbed by plantlife which in turn is eaten by deer. If the soil is low in mineral nutrients, antler growth will suffer.**

You see, by the conclusion of the rut, a buck which has run himself ragged servicing as many estrus does as he can find may have lost as much as 20 percent of his body weight. If bitter cold weather and deep snow arrive before the animal has an opportunity to regain this lost weight, he enters the long winter lean and in a state of physical deterioration. As a result, at a time of year when food is the least plentiful, the buck may eventually succumb to still additional weight loss predictably followed by exhaustion-induced pneumonia.

Consequently, if you ever spotted a mature buck carrying a heavy set of antlers, and didn't succeed in taking him, and the hunting season was immediately followed by a long and unusually severe winter, and you never saw the deer again, he's likely no longer around. While he may have been taken by another hunter on another property, or was poached at night, or perhaps came out second-best in a highway skirmish with a furniture truck, the greater likelihood is that he succumbed as a result of a rapidly deteriorating state of health.

Due to these circumstances, an increasing number of hunters and land managers are helping their deer along by improving their general overall health, ensuring that winterkill is kept to a minimum, and assisting bucks in achieving their maximum potential for large antler growth.

As we've seen, food plots that offer deer a high carbohydrate/protein intake during the spring-summer-fall period, followed by a supplemental feeding program in regions where winters are difficult for wildlife, are a splendid idea. But complementing this, numerous companies also are now producing a wide variety of mineral supplements, many of them laced with vitamins, which are designed specifically for whitetails. This two-pronged effort is not intended to entirely support deer but to simply offer them a more complete, filling, and nutritional menu than their natural range is capable of providing; just keep in mind when planning upcoming in-field projects that it's during the late-winter and early-spring months when deer need this help the most.

There also are many supplemental feeds and mineral products specifically intended for gamebirds and other wildlife species and they're discussed in later chapters).

Land managers have learned they can greatly improve the antler growth of bucks, but mineral licks must be maintained every year; otherwise, the deer experience a roller coaster ride of nutritional highs and lows.

As with established food plots, mineral supplements for deer must be provided every year or the animals will experience a roller coaster ride of nutritional highs and lows, with the lows often negating any highs which previously were gained. So once you have mineral licks established, don't be tempted to occasionally skip a year in "freshening" them with a renewed application. Each lick will adequately serve 40 acres of deer habitat, and maintaining each lick is inexpensive and takes only a few minutes of time.

Do not expect overnight results with mineral supplements. As mentioned earlier, it's only after an optimum state of health has been achieved over a period of time do excess nutrients begin finding themselves channeled into increased reproduction, increased fawn survival, and increased antler growth and development.

Consequently, it usually takes two or three years before you'll begin seeing a noticeable increase in the number of deer in your immediate area and an increase in antler size among bucks. In fact, on my own farm and on cooperating surrounding properties, we now no longer see 1-1/2 year old bucks with spikes or even forked antlers; virtually all of their first "true" antlers, after the button-buck stage, are small six- or eight-point racks!

## A CLOSER LOOK AT MINERALS

There are numerous brands of mineral supplements on the market and most companies selling them advertise in the popular deer hunting magazines; just call and request their brochures, or check the listing at the end of this chapter.

One word of caution: Don't attempt to economize by purchasing mineral supplements from feed stores because these are inexpensive brands that are intended for livestock; most of them lack copper which is toxic to sheep and cattle but essential to a whitetail deer's production of antler growth.

Deer-specific mineral supplements are available in powder, granulated, and block form, but a hunter or landowner may be at a loss as to which of the many available brands is best. Texas deer biologist Larry Weishuhn, has some definite thoughts on this subject.

"In conjunction with my research into the nutritional needs of deer, and more specifically antler development among bucks, I had friends from throughout the whitetail's range send me freshly shed antlers of various sizes," Larry explained. "We then took core samples from these antlers and did a composition analysis." Weishuhn discovered that the largest antlers were much higher in sodium, zinc and manganese than smaller antlers.

Another deer researcher, Alabama's John Martin of the Deer-Lix Company, has a slightly different opinion. His work was conducted in association with the College of Agriculture at Penn State University and it showed that phosphorus plays a vital role in the metabolism of deer.

While phosphorus is important to the growth of antlers, it also is a constituent of bones and teeth. But most important, it is necessary for calcium utilization. Calcium can only be transformed into bone and antler to the extent that the necessary proportion of phosphorus is ingested by the animal, provided, of course, that calcium is also taken in. Moreover, the

Penn State researchers say that even in regions where phosphorus and calcium are at normal levels, additional supplements of these minerals can accelerate antler and body growth to even greater levels. So good advice is to read the ingredients labels on various mineral-supplement products you may be considering, to learn which particular brands are highest in sodium, zinc, manganese, phosphorus, calcium, and copper. If you find some brands that additionally contain various combinations of potassium, cobalt, selenium, iodine, vitamins A, D, and E, and other nutrients designed to enhance skeletal development and overall body growth, all the better.

Before buying, read the product's labeling content; the mineral blend should be high in sodium, zinc, manganese, phosphorus, calcium, and copper. Minerals in powder form should be placed on a rotted stump that will absorb the product; deer then eat the soft, mineral-saturated wood and all.

For those landowners who are the most serious about their deer management programs, some companies such as the Whitetail Institute of North America, BioLogic, and Diamond Products even offer seasonal-variation mineral supplements that can be provided to their deer during the late winter/early spring, spring/summer, and fall/winter periods. During these distinct time frames, whitetails have more specific bodily needs than at other times of year but which native foods and planted foods cannot fulfill because of their own seasonal peaks; the primary variations are the predominance of high roughage content of late fall through early spring and the tender succulence of foods from late spring into fall. As a result, there's no way a single planted food-type, food supplement, or vitamin-mineral supplement can provide deer with their year-around nutritional needs.

Mineral blocks can be placed directly on the ground, but as a rule it's recommended that minerals in powder form be poured on top of a partially-rotted stump. The slowly disintegrating wood absorbs the minerals and the deer eat the soft, mineral-saturated wood and all.

Using granulated minerals is entirely different. Begin by clearing away leaves and grass to bare soil from an area of ground about three feet in diameter. Now, in the center of the clearing, dig a hole about six inches deep and 20 inches in diameter. Then pour in the bag of quantity of minerals recommended on the bag and shovel the dirt from the hole back on top. Finally, mix together the dirt and the minerals with a hoe and you're finished.

Years ago, when I created mineral licks on my land for the first time, I returned to the sites several months later and was shocked at what I found. The licks had been so aggressively pawed, and eaten

**Granular mineral products should be placed on bare soil and mixed with dirt and leaf-litter. Deer managers should establish one mineral lick for every 40 acres of land under their control.**

at, that they now measured 12 inches deep and 4 feet in diameter! Tracks profusely peppered the ground all around, and there now also was evidence of worn trails funneling into each lick like spokes to the hub of a wheel. Today, some of the licks have since been gradually enlarged by deer to six feet or more in diameter and are up to 18 inches deep, meaning that it's time for me to stop sweetening them, fill them in, and activate new licks nearby; the reason is simply to eliminate a hazardous hole someone might step into in the dark.

In little time, the lick depression created by deer, whether a block or granulated mineral supplement was initially placed there, will fill with rain water and deer no longer will eat the combined soil and minerals; they'll simply drink the highly enriched water! From that point on, "sweetening" each lick is simply a matter of adding more granulated minerals to the muddy-water hole and stirring.

The "where factor" in establishing a mineral lick is just as important as the "when" and "how" factors. Deer biologists recommend that licks be placed along trails connecting established bedding and feeding areas, simply because of the regular traffic these particular trails receive. Moreover, establish each lick in or adjacent to cover-areas as opposed to exposed, open-ground locations to encourage deer to visit the lick at any hour, rather than only at night. Also be sure to situate mineral licks in regions which do not experience much human disturbance.

**As deer repeatedly visit a mineral lick and paw at it, a depression will be created that quickly fills with rainwater. Deer continue to visit the site to drink the mineral-enriched water.**

# MINERAL/VITAMIN SOURCES

**Antler King Trophy Products**
W11353 Spaulding Rd.
Black River Falls, WI 54615
www.antlerking.com

**BioLogic**
P.O. Box 757
West Point, MS 39773
(601) 494-8859
www.mossyoak.com

**Deer Lix Mineral Supplement**
**Martin Mfg. Co.**
1742 Brown Rd.
Hephzibah, GA 30815

**Diamond Products, Inc.**
**c/o Realtree**
P.0. Box 9638
Columbus, GA 31908

**Hard Hunter**
1562 - 160th St.
Centuria, WI 54824
(800) 700-9334
mctech@win.bright.net

**Horns-A-Plenty Mineral Mix**
3831 Hereford Rd.
Erie, PA 16510

**Megabucks**
P.O. Box 2116
Sinking Spring, PA 19608
(800) 634-2282

**Mega-Rack/Temptation Lures**
N10353 City Hwy P
Iola, WI 54945

**Mossy Oak/BioLogic**
P.O. Box 757
West Point, MS 39773
(662) 494-8859
www.mossyoak.com

**Purina Mills**
P.O. Box 66812
St. Louis, MO 63166
(800) 227-8941

**Pennington Seed Co.**
Box 290
Madison, GA 30650

**Ultra Bucks Mineral**
**Supplement**
Box 311
Troy, PA 16947

**Whitetail Institute of North America**
Route 1, Box 3006
Pintlala, AL 36043
(800) 688-3030
www.deernutrition.com

# CHAPTER 13

## HOW TO HAVE
## MORE TURKEYS

According to the National Shooting Sports Foundation (NSSF), 60 percent of those who avidly hunt deer also hunt turkeys.

So it stands to reason that when managing a property with deer as the primary focus, any subtle considerations that benefit deer but also simultaneously have the effect of greatly expanding turkey populations, and improving their health, are well-worthwhile.

Happily, a great many of the forages put into food plots for deer are also eagerly fed upon by turkeys.

Let's say, for example, that you intend to put in several food plots to clover blends because it's no secret that deer relish all clover varieties.

Many food plots put in for deer also favor turkeys. Red clover, ladino clover, alfalfa, birdsfoot trefoil, rye, wheat, and soybeans are eagerly sought by both species.

Nevertheless, it would be wise to first study the seed formulations offered by various companies that sell clover blends. What you want to determine is which company-blends in particular emphasize, by percentage-of-composition, the inclusion of red clover and/or ladino clover because those two specific varieties are the favorites of turkeys.

In so doing, you get a two-fer. For the one-time investments of time and money into a given food plot, deer are drawn to your land-base, and held there, because of the simple biological tenet that "where you plant food, that's where the deer will be." But in this particular instance you also get a bonus . . . turkeys!

## OTHER FOODS FAVORED BY TURKEYS

After a long winter, the first hint of spring sees turkeys in search of vegetation. As a result, they're often concentrated in lowlands such as creek bottoms. Lower elevations are always warmer than surrounding higher ground, and they always have a much higher moisture content. As a result, they're the first locations to green-up. However, the newly emerging vegetation there, although lush, consists mostly of weed species of low nutrient value.

This is why it's a good idea, if possible, to try to incorporate either rye, winter wheat, or a variety of spring oats into a couple of food plots. Not only will deer home-in upon any of the three, but turkeys much favor these forages over even the tenderest of lowland weed vegetation.

Other grasses and legumes that turkeys dote upon include alfalfa, timothy, and birdsfoot trefoil . . . all of which, still again, are prime foods of deer. And yet others favored by both species are grain sorghum, browntop millet, corn, and soybeans.

However, while corn and soybeans are attractive to turkeys, they forage upon them at different times than deer. Deer hit the corn just when it's beginning to mature, through the curing-time that takes place in fall, and throughout the winter period. They likewise forage on the soybeans—not just the beans but also the leaves, stems, and even the roots—over the course of many months.

But turkeys concentrate the bulk of their feeding upon corn and soybeans much later in the year, for two reasons. With the plants now brown and withered, longer-range visibility can forewarn them of danger from predators. And since much of the forage has been knocked down to some extent, they can graze along and take advantage of forage that now is more easily accessible than was the case months or even weeks earlier.

We noted in a previous chapter that where corn and soybeans are not planted in food plots, landowners commonly offer them to deer through the use of mechanical feeders. Interestingly, it's quite common for deer approaching a feeder to chase away any turkeys that may already be there. But as soon as the deer finish feeding and leave, the turkeys are back in an instant! When planting soft-mast foods and fruit trees for deer as part of an overall land-management program, keep in mind that persimmons are not only highly sought after by deer but also turkeys.

The number-one food plot planting that specifically targets turkeys is chufa. Unfortunately, since it's a below-ground tuber, it isn't heavily utilized by deer; plus, chufa grows best only in the year-around warmer southern climates.

So are blackberries and raspberries; if these particular foods are native to the land-holding, it's not necessary to plant them from nursery stock, but they will spread and produce a more bountiful crop if a native-plant fertilizer such as Scott's is periodically applied.

Finally, serious hunters know that food plots planted to chufa are highly attractive to turkeys and deer alike. Most have the erroneous belief that chufa grows well only in the deep South. Actually, however, it is easily grown from Florida to Canada, as long as the ground in a given region does not stay frozen for extended periods of time.

Chufa is a grass-like sedge that grows up to two feet tall. But while turkeys and deer forage upon its leaves, both species particularly favor the peanut-like tubers the plants produce underground. The tubers average 1/2 inch in diameter and 1-inch in length and are shallow, just beneath the surface of the soil, where deer and turkeys can easily paw and scratch them up for consumption.

In most regions, the recommended planting time for chufa is May through August, depending upon latitude. The tubers are planted no more than two inches deep, in row-crop fashion the same as soybeans. Only moderate fertilization is required, chiefly nitrogen, with a recommended application rate being 250 pounds per acre of 13-13-13.

Chufa is both an annual and a perennial. Ideally, for maximum forage production, it should be replanted every year. But if you don't get around to it some year, it will partially volunteer for another year or two.

One word of caution. Raccoons will quickly and entirely devastate a chufa food plot smaller than a half acre. So the rule of thumb is twofold: Be sure the immediate region does not have a high raccoon population, or ensure the chufa food plot is at least three acres in size.

## BOOSTING THEIR NUMBERS

It's been said that if you can make habitat areas attractive to hen turkeys, and enhance their reproduction rate, the gobbler part of the equation will take care of itself.

In early spring, hens gravitate toward brushy thickets where they can eventually find nesting sites, so in one's attempt to provide deer with maximum feeding opportunities, remember to keep a certain percentage of the land-base in " scrub" woody vegetation. Hens lay from 8 to 16 eggs, with the average being 12. Of the eggs laid and successfully incubated and hatched, 20 percent of the chicks are lost to wet, cold weather. An additional 30 percent are lost as a result of being preyed upon by coyotes, foxes, raccoons, bobcats, and free-roaming dogs and housecats.

There's nothing a land manager can do about weather losses, but he can sharply increase their numbers by reducing the predation problem. The first order of business is to find the nesting sites. The peak nesting time is late-March to mid-June, depending upon latitude, and the nests generally are located on lee slopes somewhat protected from the prevailing wind direction and in brushy-cover areas.

Strive to maintain a number of brushy thickets on your acreage that will serve as turkey nesting habitat. Immediately after chicks have hatched, broadcast handfuls of wheat in the area because this allows poults to develop their flight feathers weeks earlier than usual and increases their survival rate by 20 percent.

So simply hike around and look for the nests which appear as saucer-shaped depressions lined with leaves and downy breast feathers. The hens, of course, will have scattered during your approach, temporarily abandoning the recently laid eggs; if they've already hatched, the chicks will scramble along after their mothers, but the hens and their brood will return to the nesting site shortly after you leave.

When you begin finding nests in a given region, sprinkle wheat on the ground but don't simply pour the feed in a pile because chicks like to find it own their own in the leaf litter by the search-and-peck method. So good advice is to carry the wheat, 30 pounds at a time, in some sort of shoulder bag, and then randomly broadcast it by the handful in the vicinity of nesting sites.

Studies have shown that when turkey poults are given this high-nutrient food supplement they develop their flight feathers a full two weeks earlier than otherwise, allowing them to fly up onto low tree branches at the first hint that a predator is approaching.

By the way, in addition to wheat, Purina makes a blend called Flight Conditioner, which is available by special order through all mills that carry Purina products.

## THE COVER CONNECTION

In a previous chapter we described the recommended treatment of the edges of interior access roads, old logging trails and powerline corridors with Arsenal herbicide to knock down hardwood brush. This results in a regenerative profusion of herbaceous foliage and a wide diversity of grasses that deer favor. But the practice also encourages the growth of wildflowers and weed species that flower-out, and these in turn produce pollen, which in turn foster heavy insect production, which in turn attract turkeys; this is important to turkey management because during the warm-weather months " bugging" constitutes as much as 30 percent of their diet intake.

Turkey roosting sites are important, too. In clear weather, they like to roost in tall, mature hardwoods that have large crowns made up of gnarly, widespread limbs; they particularly like beech trees, sycamores and oaks. But during inclement weather, they like their perches to afford a bit of protection from wind and rain and select mature conifer species.

Of course, a landowner can't do anything about tree roosting sites on a short-term basis. But he can keep all of this in mind whenever engaging in land-clearing practices and periodic selective logging. So before cutting certain trees in certain areas, think the matter through because judiciously leaving specific trees in place may contribute to your overall wildlife management plan by providing ideal turkey roosting sites. As a side benefit, certain species of preferred hardwood roosting trees yield still other benefits on behalf of turkeys and deer by bearing bountiful crops of two of their favorite forages . . . beechnuts and acorns.

At the approach of inclement weather, turkeys like to retreat into weather-sheltered conifer plantations; you have an ongoing tree-planting program, don't you?

When it comes to their strutting grounds, gobblers have solid preferences. Places where relatively thin woods and grassy, open areas meet are especially attractive to them because in their attempt to locate hens they want to be able to see a long distance, and likewise make themselves highly visible. As a result, gobblers like to hang around slightly elevated knolls, open saddles in wooded areas, small clearings off to the sides of old logging roads, creek bottoms, and open woodlands bordered by brushy terrain where hens are likely to seek nesting sites.

So this insight, too, is worth keeping in mind when planning both food plots and timber-management programs.

# CHAPTER 14

## MANAGING FOR
# UPLAND GAMEBIRDS

Of the many gamebird species that inhabit North America, doves, quail, pheasant and ruffed grouse in particular are attracted to food plantings and benefit from them. And happily, many of their preferred foods are the same as those planted more specifically for deer and turkeys. In fact, some foods are so universal in their appeal to game and other wildlife that you never know what to expect to show up.

I remember one time I hiked to one of my food plots to enjoy an afternoon of dove hunting. The patch was planted to browntop millet and as I approached the field edge a covey of quail suddenly burst into flight. Not at all expecting this, I just stood there and watched them glide into a distant crabapple thicket. After sitting down on my stool, I waited a full hour before any doves began filtering into my area. But I wasn't bored for a minute because a flock of turkeys that had wandered into the food plot provided a good show as they strutted and squabbled among themselves. Then shortly after the turkeys departed, a whitetail doe and her two yearlings arrived for lunch.

Unfortunately, native gamebird populations are down almost everywhere because in recent decades much of their preferred habitat has been lost to both development and so-called "clean" farming practices.

So when anyone tells me they've recently acquired a piece of land in the country, and they ask what they can do to improve gamebird populations, I usually say "do nothing!"

What I mean is, they shouldn't be so eager to put in food plots that they

In regions that have become depleted of native gamebirds, many land managers raise their own in captivity and release them to increase self-sustaining populations. In select regions, state wildlife departments sell or assist in such release programs.

unceremoniously bush-hog every brushy thicket, mow down every grassy swale, tear out every grown-over fencerow, and backfill every culvert and ditch.

Gamebirds need places to nest, rear their young, hide from predators, and find shelter from severe weather. As a result, "cover" is actually more important to them than any food plots a landowner can plant. Granted, all critters must eat, and highly preferred foods will attract gamebirds to specific places. But the food alone won't permanently hold them on a given property. Cover does that! So attend to their cover needs first, and then their food, in that order, and there's a good chance gamebirds indigenous to that part of the country will move in and establish themselves.

Even still, some regions may be so depleted of native gamebirds that many landowners decide to jump-start their wildlife management programs by propagating their own birds for release.

Doves and ruffed grouse are not raised in captivity. But breeders that sell quail and pheasant chicks (and even eggs for incubation) advertise in the classified ads in sportsmen's magazines and ship birds to all regions of the country; some farm-supply outlets also have contacts with gamebird breeders.

Upon delivery, the birds are then raised on the grounds to either the poult or adult stage and then released to create a self-sustaining population. The key to the success of these efforts is to have already-existing cover when the birds are released so they may quickly and easily adapt to their new homes. If food plots also are already in place, all to the good, but if they haven't yet been established, the birds will do

Gamebirds raised in captivity are widely available from breeders. They can be purchased as eggs to be incubated or as two-week-old poults; in either case, the birds are fed high-nutrition food and vitamin supplements to about 8 weeks of age before being released.

okay during the meanwhile by feeding upon native weed seeds and bugs.

Purina Mills has an has an excellent gamebird management booklet (free) that describes everything one needs to know about incubating and hatching eggs, raising chicks to the poult and adult stages with their recommended feeding and nutrition program, and rearing-equipment guidelines, to ensure healthy birds that upon release quickly "go wild" and adapt to the habitat.

## HOW TO IMPROVE YOUR QUAIL HUNTING

Fortunately, quail don't move around. They occupy relatively small home ranges, are very adaptable, and therefore are ideal gamebirds to manage on small amounts of acreage.

For bobwhites, food plots no more than one-half acre in size are recommended. Ideal sites are small, tight, sun-drenched openings in piney woods, hardwoods, fire breaks, cutovers, swamp perimeters, or other hard-to-reach areas. In any of these places where you might be thinking of putting in food

plots for deer, you might want to consider a planting

In putting in food plots that are attractive to deer but more specifically intended for gamebirds, keep in mind they favor lespedeza, millet, sorghum, clover, wheat, oats, and corn. Also, strip-cropping, with alternating rows of different food varieties, is much better than a single larger plot planted to just one food-type.

that's also attractive to quail. They highly favor Korean lespedeza, browntop millet, beggarweed, partridge peas, grain sorghum, clover, Egyptian wheat, and oats. Once any of these small-grain varieties are well-established, periodic strip-disking is very beneficial to the species.

Reseeding soybeans, such as the Quail Haven variety, also are popular among land managers. I first learned about this planting from my friend Tom Baker, who owns Buck Hollow Ranch near Pocahantas, Arkansas. This particular forage is planted in the same manner as regular soybeans (as described in Chapter 10) and produces an abundance of small, hard seeds that mature in late October. Those seeds which aren't eaten will over-winter and germinate again the following spring. Since it's a legume that fixes its own nitrogen, the most common recommended fertilizer is the same as for other legumes. Be sure of course to have a soil test analyzed, but likely as not you'll find it will call for about 250 pounds per acre of 0-20-20.

While we said most quail-oriented food plots should be relatively small, putting in Quail Haven reseeding soybeans is the one exception to the rule.

In best-managing gamebird habitat, especially for quail, controlled burning is an excellent management tool because it eliminates ground thatch. This makes seeds, nuts and berries more readily accessible, but always do this under the supervision of your forestry advisor.

They are so highly favored by deer that they must be planted in food plots no smaller than two acres or deer will quickly decimate them and leave nothing for the bobwhites. The one shortcoming of Quail Haven is that it grows best throughout the South. North of the Mason-Dixon line, its success is spotty.

With all other quail plantings, the seeds are small and planted shallow, just like clover as described in Chapter 7. This includes not only soil-planting of the seeds during the warm-weather months but also top-seeding them on top of snow-cover in winter; the following spring you'll have a lush crop that will immediately begin attracting bobwhites.

Controlled burning once every 4 years is an excellent management tool for quail. The place to do this is woodland areas more than 15 years of age because at this stage of growth they are beginning to shade-out the understory, reducing both food and cover. In some cases old fields also are burned if they've acquired a heavy layer of thatch on the ground. Burning eliminates thatch and hardwood brush; this is important because quail are surface-ground-feeders that eat primarily seeds and if covered by just one inch of ground-litter they are essentially unavailable to the birds.

The procedure also is called "prescribed" burning because unlike a wild-fire it is done under highly controlled conditions, typically in late winter or early spring, and in accordance with optimum humidity levels and wind direction. While the ground is left blackened, in just ten days or so a profusion of lush, regenerative greenery will sprout. A controlled burn should always be done under the supervision of your local state forester.

In still other situations, herbiciding exotic grasses such as fescue and bahia, both of which were probably originally planted for pastureland but have no food or habitat value for quail, is recommended. A non-selective herbicide such as RoundUp is the most common choice, followed by lightly disking under the dead residue before planting.

## HOW TO IMPROVE YOUR PHEASANT HUNTING

Ringneck pheasants are known as "rovers." They're eternally on the move in search of food and cover, but once they find it they stay put!

As a result, even moreso than quail, establishing cover first, followed immediately by making food available, is the best way to attract local birds to your land holding. It's also critical when rearing ringnecks incubated from eggs or purchased as chicks from a breeder. I know one individual who purchased 25 ringneck chicks, raised them in a pen to adulthood, even-tually turned them loose on his property, and never saw a single one again!

In spring, ringnecks like to nest in grassy areas. So if food plots are being put in primarily for deer, and the land manager wants pheasants as a bonus, he should probably plant a legume such as alfalfa or an alfalfa-clover blend. This goes back to what we said in Chapters 7 and 8 about it being necessary to periodically mow such food plots to reduce weed competition. But if ringneck hens are nesting in and around the food plot, you'll not want to destroy those nests. The rule of thumb, north of the Mason-Dixon line, is to mow before May 15th or after July 15th; south of the Mason-Dixon line,

Gamebird food plots attract pheasants, but it's cover that holds them in those specific areas when they're not feeding. So don't be so aggressive in intensively manicuring your acreage that you eliminate tall weeds, brushy areas, thick stands of native shrubs, roadside cover, ditches, and grown-over fencerows.

mow before April 15th or after June 15th. By planting a fast-growing legume such as alfalfa, it's ready for mowing during these specific time frames and, thus, ringneck nesting sites will not be destroyed.

Ditch banks, road-sides, and other odds areas that grow up in tall grasses and hard-wood brush also are favored nesting sites for ringnecks. So if herbicide applications are periodically under-taken in such areas, to foster the growth of native plantlife, the best time to do it is after mid-July.

During the other months of the year, the same types of shrubby and brushy cover that are attractive to bobwhites are attractive to ringnecks. One type of cover highly favored by pheasants but seldom used by quail are tight stands of cattails in lowland areas that are perpetually wet, so never destroy such stands of cover. Food plots should be planted right up to the edges of dense cover. Although the birds sometimes range far out into the middle areas of grainfields, any degree of hunting pressure cause them to quickly relocate for the remainder of the season to the edges, provided that they can find suitable food and cover there.

The favorite planted foods of ringnecks are grain sorghum, buckwheat, sunflowers, and corn. Corn in particular is their mainstay during cold winter months, particularly after harsh winds have knocked it down into "stubble" and the food is more easily accessible.

When an unexpected, early winter storm is forecast, many land managers intentionally drive their ATVs through their corn food plots to create "feeding aisles." In so doing, corridors of food are made available, while adjacent edges of still-standing corn reduce the effect of snow-drift that otherwise would cover much of the corn knocked to the ground.

## HOW TO IMPROVE YOUR DOVE HUNTING

Across the Midwest and into the southernmost states, landowners see highs and lows in their mourning dove populations as the months progress. The reason is because these regions have native birds that remain all year due to the favorable food and resting areas available to them in climate situations that do not become too severe or prolonged during the winter months. Yet these regions also see migratory birds that periodically pass through during the fall and early-winter months as they steadily retreat southward to escape from the predictably severe winter conditions settling down upon the northern-most border states.

How large the native population of doves is likely to be, and how long the migratory birds can be expected to linger before resuming their journey southward, depends upon the food made available to them and the presence of suitable roosting cover.

Unlike other gamebirds, doves don't nest in ground cover but rather in trees, the same as songbirds, so planting and maintenance of food plots at any time of year won't disturb their nesting activities.

Doves are particularly attracted to food plots planted to sunflowers, wheat, buckwheat, grain sorghum, millet, and corn. Yet they don't spend much time in or around typical ground cover where they can't see well enough to monitor their immediate

Doves are attracted to food plots planted to sunflowers, corn, wheat, buckwheat, sorghum, and millet. But to hold them there, the planting should be lightly disked after the crop matures to make the food accessible. To hold doves near feeding areas, situate food plots adjacent to stands of trees the birds need for midday resting and night-time roosting.

surroundings, preferring instead to remain on open patches of bare dirt or in low-growing food plots. For this reason, standing corn and even the small grains are often disked to knock them down, thus making the food more readily accessible and also reducing its height. In addition to providing the type of feeding situations that doves like, disking also exposes soil where doves—in fact, all gamebirds—like to "dust" and scratch for grit that aids in grinding seed-foods in their gizzards.

The cover which doves insist upon, but isn't really "cover" by strict definition, is the presence of trees they can roost in during midday resting periods and at night. During the daylight hours, when they're not feeding, they prefer dead, leaf-less trees with many branches. At night, they prefer to roost in conifers.

## HOW TO HAVE MORE RUFFED GROUSE

Grouse (in the northern border states they're commonly called "partridge" or "pat") are far more attuned to wooded habitat than other gamebird species. They particularly like brushy areas and second-growth timber.

Due to their environmental preferences, a landowner wanting more ruffed grouse can accomplish more by managing his habitat than by planting food plots; although grouse occasionally visit the edge of a field planted to corn or some other small grain, the species prefers to forage upon native foods such as wild grape, greenbrier, dogwood, aspen, hawthorn, sumac, acorns, beechnuts, and even poison ivy.

**Ruffed grouse are better woodland-habitat managed than food-managed. They prefer uneven-aged stands of mixed species of hardwoods and softwoods.**

There are only three food-types that landowners typically plant to specifically benefit ruffed grouse. Apple and dogwood trees, for their flowers, buds and fruits, are highly favored by grouse. And woodland trails and access-road edges should be planted to any variety of clover, which grouse utilize as a favored vegetation forage year around. It's a common practice among those who put in clover or clover-

Ruffed grouse eat a wide variety of native foods, especially nuts, seeds, tender tree buds, berries, and flowering fruit trees. They also favor planted clover but they don't spend much time around clover food plots. It is better to plant clover on the edges of interior access trails through woodland cover by top-seeding it on snow cover during the winter months.

blend food plots during the warm-weather months to save any leftover seed. Later in the year, when there is snow cover on the ground, they hike their trails and interior access roads through woodland areas and broadcast spread the seed on top of the snow. As the winter progresses, the seed percolates down through the snow to the ground; when the soil begins to warm in spring, the seed quickly germinates and provides a lush carpet of greenery that the birds relish.

However, the best overall management technique for ruffed grouse is maintaining uneven-aged stands of woodland growth. Periodic timber harvesting practices open the forest canopy to stimulate the growth of shrubby cover, woody vines, and regenerative saplings that yield a cornucopia of tender leaves, seeds, berries and buds.

For night-roosting cover, and protection from severe weather, ruffed grouse distinctly prefer blocks of closely-planted conifers situated on lee hillsides and which have thick branches that touch each other.

# SOURCES FOR SEEDS & MORE INFORMATION

**Adams-Briscoe Seed Co.**
P.O. Box 19
Jackson, GA 30233
(770) 775-7826
abseed@juno.com

**C.P. Daniels**
**& Sons Seed Co.**
Box 119
Waynesboro, GA 30830

**Purina Mills**
1401 S. Hanley Rd.
St. Louis, MO 63114
(800) 227-8941

**Quail Unlimited**
P.O. Box 610
Edgefield, SC 29824
(803) 637-5731
www.qu.org

**Ruffed Grouse Society**
451 McCormick Rd.
Coraopolis, PA 15108
(412) 262-4044
www.ruffedgrousesociety.org

**Tall Timbers**
**Quail Research Station**
13093 Henry Beadel Dr.
Tallahassee, FL 32312
(850) 893-4153

# CHAPTER 15

## MANAGING FOR
# MORE SMALL GAME

The term "wildlife" commonly brings to mind deer and gamebirds. But actually, the number of rabbits and squirrels taken annually by hunters far outnumber all otherspecies. Rabbits and squirrels provide enjoyable sport and delicious eating. And they're excellent species to go after when introducing youngsters to hunting, thesafe handling of firearms, woodsmanship, and being good stewards of the land.

## HOW TO HAVE MORE RABBITS

Most of what we'll have to say here deals with cottontails, which are found nationwide. In the more arid regions of the west there also are jackrabbits, and in the colder northern and high-elevation climes there also are hares, but both are far less manageable than cottontails.

Cottontails prefer relatively open ground closely bordered by thickets, brush and tall grass and they use so-called "travel lanes" to get back and forth between feeding and resting areas; a travel lane usually is a

Cottontails thrive almost everywhere but there are certain deer food plots that also highly favor rabbits. They'll become frequent visitors to the outer perimeters of plantings made to brassica, clover, corn, wheat, and soybeans.

narrow corridor of sorts where there is bare ground snaking through tall cover, but it also may be an "edge" such as a fencerow, stream bank, drainage ditch, or the border of a field.

Cottontails are herbivores and they forage almost exclusively upon green plants early in the year. Then, upon the onset of cold weather when most plantlife slips into a dormant stage, they switch to "woody" browse such as the bark of young trees and brush, roots that are near the surface, and twigs and stems that are within reach.

Because cottontails have a wide-ranging acceptance of most native foods that exist in their home ranges, few land managers plant foods specifically for rabbits. But if you have a choice among various food plot plantings, and you're multi-species oriented, keep in mind that rabbits distinctly favor the following plantings: Clover, corn, wheat, soybeans, and leafy members of the brassica family (turnips, cabbage, mustard, chicory).

One landowner I know is so enthusiastic about rabbit hunting that he strives for optimum populations and intentionally plants food plots for the species. They're always tiny plots, less than one-quarter acre and therefore not as suitable for deer, and he plants them in perennial clover mixed with cereal grain; an example might be a blend of white clover with either oats, wheat, or rye.

However, most rabbit "management" techniques involve their habitat; if the habitat is ideal, rabbit populations will dramatically increase and there should be little problem with them finding enough to eat. Native foods cottontails prefer include curly dock, sheep sorrel, plaintains, wild carrot, clover, prickly lettuce, giant ragweed, and chicory. They also favor woody plants such as newly-emerging sumac, willow, crabapple, maple shoots, and

Rabbits cling to thickets, briars, and brushy ground cover. In winter, they seek shelterbelts of mixed woody cover where they eat the bark and exposed roots of young trees and shrubs.

blackberry; in all cases they eat the tender leaves and buds in spring and summer, and in winter switch to the twigs, bark and exposed roots.

The best way to improve native-food opportunities for rabbits is to selectively cut brushy areas as the canopy begins to shade out weeds and grasses. But don't entirely mow or herbicide large

NORTH-COUNTRY WHITETAILS

In the absence of thickets and woody cover for rabbit habitat, create your own when engaging in timber-stand improvement by cutting living brush piles. Saw undesirable trees only partway through and let them fall with their trunks still attached to the stumps.

blocks of cover; much better is to cut or spray random aisles. Don't worry about the rabbits' need for water. In warm, wet weather, they drink from puddles and ditches, and in winter they eat snow. During periods of drought, they're able to metabolize moisture from the vegetation and browse they eat.

There are several ways to improve so-called "loafing," hiding, and nesting areas for rabbits. First, always leave intact brushy fencerows, weedy drainage ditches and shrubby dry culverts. But also, consider creating "living brush piles" during TSI (timber-stand improvement). When selectively removing trees that have little reachable food value to wildlife, and no commercial value to you, don't saw their trunks all the way through and close to the ground. Saw them several feet off the ground, and only partway through, just enough for the tree to fall and yet remain attached by a "hinge" to its trunk. In this manner, the tree will remain alive for many years, as it is able to still suck moisture and nutrients out of the ground via the mother trunk's root complex. Moreover, the crown of the tree now is laying on the ground, providing rabbits (and deer and turkeys) with year-around bushy cover and easy feeding opportunities upon twigs, buds, flowers, and seeds.

In other cases, let's say you decide to fell a certain number of trees which have no wildlife or commercial value but you intend to reduce the trunk and larger limbs to firewood. Simply go about this task as you usually do, but create rabbit cover in the process by stacking up the smaller limbs into brush piles.

For optimum rabbit hiding and denning conditions, the brush piles should be 5 feet high and 15 feet in diameter and of relatively loose construction; this

After a timber harvest, pile up the cull branches to provide "hutches" that will quickly become occupied by rabbits.

will give rabbits an advantage in evading predators such as foxes and raptors such as hawks and owls. But also, to ensure the brush pile has longevity, establish it on a base-framework of several large-diameter limbs to prevent the pile from settling too tight on the surface of the ground and quickly deteriorating. A rabbit "hide" constructed in this manner will remain functional for about 10 years.

## HOW TO HAVE MORE SQUIRRELS

Fox squirrels and gray squirrels live nationwide, and they both have many color interphases that range from amber to red to melanistic (black).

Although squirrels occasionally nibble upon green plantlife and tender, newly emerging buds and twigs, their primary forage is hard mast (nuts and seeds). When seasonally available, they also feed heavily upon so-called soft mast such as wild grapes, plums, cherries, crabapples, and mushrooms.

In managing squirrel habitat, you can't do much to provide them with their preferred hardwood mast-producing trees if they don't already exist; it can take 40 years or longer for nature to attend to this task. But you can, through TSI, enhance squirrel habitat which already exists to make it more attractive to still larger numbers of bushytails; this works off the simple principle that squirrels are territorial, so if you expand and improve upon their preferred food sources and denning sites you thus allow their numbers to increase.

First, regarding food availability, and when cutting trees for a timber sale or firewood, strive to retain a modest percentage of oaks, and especially hickories, that are at least 12 inches in diameter, as these are the most prolific mast-producers. The recommended rate of preservation is 35 trees per acre and at a ratio of 1:10 (that is, a one-acre block for every 10 acres of mature forestland).

Also, when engaging in various land-clearing practices in forestland areas inhabited by squirrels, do not kill grapevines, blackberries, persimmons, wild cherry, hawthorne and dogwood as these are important food sources during years when hard-mast production is low; many of these forage varieties also are favored by deer, turkey and various gamebirds.

In regions distinctly absent of soft-mast foods, planting an apple tree at a rate of 1:20 (one tree for every 20 acres) also is very beneficial; any of the dwarf apple-tree varieties begin bearing fruit in as little as only three years.

The denning habits of both gray and fox squirrels is primarily in large, ageing hardwoods, particularly beech trees. Ideally (from the squirrels' standpoint) there will be either holes or cavities in the trunks that give access to interior chambers the squirrels can line with dry leaves. So strive to retain any beeches that are evident, especially those of at least 24 inches in diameter. In optimum squirrel habitat, there should be three den sites per acre.

In the absence of such holes and cavities, squirrels construct two-foot diameter leaf nests in the forks and crotches of any species of a mature tree's sprawling limb structure. But a leaf nest is not their denning preference, mainly because it's not as weatherproof as a trunk cavity. In this situation, land managers commonly make their own squirrel den structures and hang them in the vicinity of hardwood mast-producing trees at a distribution rate of about three structures per acre.

The primary forage of squirrels is hard mast. The only food plots they occasionally visit are those planted to corn. So increasing squirrel populations should be oriented to forest management of trees that bear nuts and seeds.

One type of squirrel den box that's easily constructed can be made from scrap lumber. In size, it should resemble a breadbox standing on end with a sloping roof and a 3-inch diameter entrance hole near the top of one of the sides. The bottom (floor) of the structure should not be solid wood but

No matter how much hard mast is available to squirrels, they won't be present in high numbers without suitable denning habitat. If there's no evidence of old trees with holes and cavities in their trunks, inexpensive denning structures can be made from old tires and scrap lumber.

rather a piece of 1/2-inch wire mesh stapled in place. The den box can then be nailed or wired right against the tree trunk; place it so the entrance hole is away from the prevailing wind, preferably at least 25 feet off the ground, and near a solid limb.

Far less expensive and time-consuming is making denning structures from old tires. Each tire will make two dens by cutting them in half with tin shears, folding them back upon themselves as shown in the diagram, and then hanging them from a high tree limb with a stout length of wire.

One study conducted by The Wildlife Society revealed that when natural tree-cavity den sites are absent from an area, and squirrels are forced to construct leaf nests, they almost instantly abandon those leaf nests and take up new residences when wooden or tire dens are provided by the land manager. The reason is because such manmade dens afford much better protection from the weather and the survival rate of newborn squirrels is three times as high.

Unlike rabbits, which are able to metabolize water from their predominantly green forage, squirrels need to periodically drink. As a result, in periods of extreme prolonged drought, they often migrate many miles in search of water and in so doing ultimately adopt new home ranges.

In regions that periodically experience severe, prolonged droughts, land managers commonly retain their squirrel populations by ensuring drinking sources in the same manner as those managing primarily for deer; these suggestions are described in Chapter 3.

# CHAPTER 16

## MANAGING FOR
# MORE DUCKS & GEESE

Few wildlife species make themselves more visible to landowners, and are of greater delight to watch and listen to as their wings sing against the night sky, than geese. Second place goes to various species of ducks. Even if you don't hunt them, simply having them around is a pleasure.

And you can indeed have them around during their migratory times of year, and in some cases as year-around residents, through a few simple types of habitat manipulation that benefits their specific needs.

How successful you'll be hinges upon several factors; the most important being nesting habitat and the presence of food. Water is also a plus that, in itself, isn't absolutely critical but does distinctly tilt the odds in your favor. But "cover," in the traditional sense, is unimportant.

Flights of wildfowl winging overhead are one of the special pleasures enjoyed by those who own or lease land. With certain management practices, you can enjoy having them stay year-around or at least delay their quick migratory pass-throughs.

Expect little success, however, if you own or lease highland ground consisting mostly of forestland. One exception in which marginal success can be enjoyed in mountainous terrain is if you have at least a few plateau situations where food plots can be put in and other terrain situations that lend themselves to the construction of one or more ponds.

Better success is bestowed on behalf of those who own or lease any low-elevation, hardwood bottomland where there are year-around streams or a river that periodically run over their banks during spring flooding periods.

Still better success can be expected if you have so-called wetlands where low-elevation areas of the property serve little more than as catch-basins for rainfall and therefore have either standing water or they remain perpetually damp year-around. Add to the picture a pond or two on the property and the landowner will come to believe he lives in waterfowl heaven.

## HOW TO MANAGE FOR MORE GEESE

It's been said, "Be careful what you wish for, for your wish may come true." And the fact of the matter is that in many regions Canada geese in particular have become so numerous they've almost achieved pest status. But for our purposes of discussion here, we'll assume the land manager has no geese at all and wants to attract them, hopefully only in modest numbers.

When it comes to their preferred foods, Canada geese are opportunists. They relish aquatic vegetation such as wild rice, wild celery, newly emerging reeds, marsh grass, and a wide variety of shallow pre-emergent vegetation (that which has sprouted and is growing upward but hasn't yet reached the surface). Geese also eagerly feed upon clover, alfalfa and other grasses, as anyone who has recently visited a golf course is well aware.

If a clover planting is intended and the ground is damp for much of the year, go with the webfoot clover variety. This is a special strain that is wetness-tolerant, but since it is not as competitive as the other clover strains, or alfalfa, use double the recommended seeding rate. Webfoot is a perennial that should give you a good stand for five years; it's also a member of the legume family and therefore requires liming to lower the soil pH to 7.0 or slightly below.

However, given any choice among various food-types, geese feed especially heavy upon grain whenever it's available. Consequently, corn, soybeans, oats, wheat, barley, millet and sorghum are high on their hit list. This is especially the case if the particular grain has cured-out (matured and dried) and then been knocked down in some manner, most commonly by once running over it lightly with a disk.

In the spring, geese seek out nesting habitat and its presence, or lack of it, determines whether they'll stop on your property. The presence of food, then, determines how long they'll stay.

If nesting habitat is not artificially provided by the land manager, geese like to find grassy hummocks adjacent to sources of water. If such natural habitat is not present to a great extent, a landowner can inexpensively create so-called nesting tubs that Canadas will readily use. By "tubs" we mean exactly that . . . old wash tubs or even the sawed-off bottom sections of 55 gallon steel drums or plastic barrels. In open, shallow-water areas the recommended procedure is to place them on small, three-foot-square wooden structures just above the surface of the water and line them with straw.

In wetland habitat where there are perpetually damp areas, mud flats, or very shallow water, the tubs can be placed directly on the mud, held in place with upright sections of old pipe to prevent them from blowing away if the water level rises and the wind kicks up; the poles should be attached through makeshift sleeves attached to the sides of the tubs so the tub can rise or fall in accordance with changing water levels.

As a rule, nest tubs should be within 20 to 30 feet of dry land but, most important, at least 200 yards apart if they are in view of each

Having geese year-around hinges upon the availability of nesting habitat. If there are no natural, grassy hummocks adjacent to water, they'll readily adapt to manmade nests. One type is made from old wash tubs.

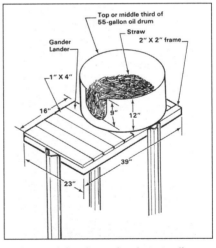

A more labor-intensive, but sturdier, goose-nesting device is a metal or plastic barrel sawed in half and anchored to a platform just above the surface of the water.

other, to minimize territorial conflicts between nesting pairs of geese. However, if visual barriers exist, such as the curvature of the shoreline or tall reeds, the tubs can be placed as close as 100 yards to each other.

## HOW TO MANAGE FOR MORE DUCKS

Some type of standing water is essential for attracting and holding ducks. Preferably, this will be a large shallow pond or a wide, winding, slow-moving stream or river. But it can also be a wetland area that periodically floods lowland timbered areas and results in shallow, standing water for many weeks of the year.

Yet even with this ideal habitat, most duck species that stop-over will make only brief visits before continuing on. The two exceptions are wood ducks and mallards (also called "greenheads"), both of which both are far more amenable to a landowner's efforts to keep them around.

As a rule, mallards are the same as geese in that they use the same types of tall shoreline grass for nesting. If these conditions aren't prevalent, land managers commonly make their own so-called nest cylinders.

To make a nest cylinder, cut a seven-foot length of 36-inch-wide fencing wire; a standard 50-foot roll will therefore make seven nests. The finished result of each nest will be a cylinder of wire mesh that is 36 inches long by 12 inches in diameter. But the key to its success as a mallard nesting site is placing handfuls of dry grass on the wire as it's being rolled into the cylinder; thus, several layers of the matted grass are trapped and in held in place between several layers of the wire mesh. Don't attempt to use straw as it deteriorates too quickly. Dry field grass of any hay variety (such as timothy, orchardgrass or sudan) works well, but the cylinders should be dis-assembled and the grass replaced every three years.

When the cylinder is rolled, secure it at several points with short pieces of wire twisted closed at the ends.

A mallard nest cylinder should be placed over water

Mallards, and to a lesser extent wood ducks, are the most common species on private lands. They're also the most adaptable to management efforts. Both feed heavily upon aquatic vegetation and hard mast. But they'll also regularly visit deer food plots that are planted to corn, Japanese millet, and grain sorghum.

on a wooden platform that is a minimum of three feet above the highest water level expected in the spring, and it should be situated perpendicular to the prevailing wind direction to prevent the grass matting from being blown away. Also, place each nest at least 25 yards from the shoreline to minimize damage by predators. The platform upon which the nest is secured (with wire) should ideally be about 8 inches wide by three feet in length and mounted on an approximate six-foot length of 2 X 4, steel pipe or fence post pounded securely into in the soft bottom.

With a minimum of seven such nests in place, land managers will find themselves amazed at how readily mallards adopt

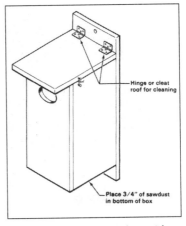

Hinge or cleat roof for cleaning

Place 3/4" of sawdust in bottom of box

**Wood ducks commonly nest in tree cavities. If these are not available, they'll readily use manmade nesting boxes similar to those made for squirrels.**

them. Moreover, once the hatchlings have grown to adulthood they'll remain in the vicinity and each spring search for their own, similar nesting sites in nearby natural cover, thus creating an impressive self-sustaining population of ducks.

Wood ducks most commonly nest in tree cavities. If such habitat is not available, they'll move on until they find it. Consequently, a land manager can build a good population of woodies by first simply providing nesting sites made from scrap lumber. Coincidentally, these nesting boxes can be of the same exterior dimensions as those made for squirrels, as described in Chapter 15. But there are a couple of exceptions.

While the entrance hole to a squirrel nesting box should be round and 2 inches in diameter, the entrance hole to a wood duck nesting box should be oval-shaped and it should be 3 inches high by 4 inches wide.

Moreover, the box should be lined with several handfuls of coarse sawdust. And the slanting roof should be mounted with hinges so the lid can be lifted and the previous year's bedding material removed and fresh sawdust added; this is not necessary with squirrels as they like to line their own nests with dry leaves and from season to season are more fastidious housekeepers than woodies.

Wood duck nesting boxes can be placed over water, on upright posts, provided they are at least six feet above the surface of the water. But wood duck boxes also can be placed in woodland habitat, attached to tree trunks, at least 10 feet off the ground and as far as several hundred yards from the nearest water source. However, since the hen must lead her ducklings to water after they hatch, there should be an aisle or unobstructed corridor of sorts between the nesting box and the water with no intervening obstacles such as a tightly-woven fence, impenetrable cover, or heavily-used county road to impede their travel.

When it comes to the feeding habits of ducks, mallards and woodies are "dabblers" that just slightly dip their head below the water's surface to feed (as opposed to "divers" which take their entire body below water to feed). Therefore, they commonly feed upon the same types of aquatic vegetation as geese, especially wild celery.

With regards to both geese and ducks, if a pond's aquatic vegetation is minimal, it can be dramatically increased by simply lowering the pond's water-elevation level by three feet during the winter and then throwing random handfuls of triple-13 fertilizer on the exposed mud flats. The following spring, an immense amount of greenery will sprout, and the water can then be allowed to return to its former level.

Adult woodies additionally feed heavily upon forestland hard mast such as small acorns and seeds. They also feed at every opportunity upon soft mast that has fallen to the ground, such as crabapples and persimmons. Conversely, hens during the egg-laying time of spring, and their newly hatched ducklings, feed almost exclusively upon protein-rich insects, spiders and small snails.

As with geese, mallards and wood ducks also feed heavily upon grain if it's made available to them in food plots that may primarily be put in for deer and upland gamebirds. However, if you decide to emphasize waterfowl feeding opportunities, keep in mind that mallards and woodies distinctly prefer Japanese millet, corn, and grain sorghum.

---

## FOR MORE DUCK & GOOSE INFORMATION

**Delta Waterfowl Foundation**
P.O. Box 3128
Bismarck, ND 58502
(701) 223-4645
www.deltawaterfowl.org

**Ducks Unlimited**
One Waterfowl Way
Memphis, TN 38120
(901) 758-3937
www.ducks.org

# CHAPTER 17

# PREDATOR CONTROL

There's a harsh, and sad, reality of any wildlife management program. Many predators lurk in the shadows and will take every opportunity to kill the wildlife you've invested so much time, expense and effort into nurturing.

## DEALING WITH TWO-LEGGED PREDATORS

Be prepared to occasionally have disreputable individuals begin taking an interest in the big-antlered bucks they may have seen from a distance in any of your food plots that are visible from the roads. If they decide to make a return visit to relieve you of one of those deer, it will undoubtedly be after dark when the animals are especially vulnerable to the use of spotlights and illegal firearms. This activity cannot be entirely eliminated, but it can be sharply reduced.

First, and most important, never personally confront someone committing an offense on your land. Keep in mind this individual has in his possession a loaded firearm, he's a criminal, he's in the process of breaking the law, and he's doing so in a relatively remote region. So this clearly is not a desirable position to put yourself in, especially after dark.

Much wiser is to simply keep your eyes and ears alert at all times to any goings-on and then quickly alert your local law enforcement agency. However, it has been my experience that calling a state game warden does not produce favorable results. At least, not immediately. These dedicated people are thinly spread across many miles of territory assigned to them, they're sorely overworked, and they're simply not able to quickly respond

There are two types of predators that can cause serious set-backs to one's wildlife management efforts. It's best to let law enforcement personnel deal with the two-legged variety.

to each and every incident involving a potential wildlife violation.

So if you see spotlights being panned across any of your food plots late at night, sure, let the warden know of the occurrence. "Maybe" in evenings to come, if he has no other pressing matters, he'll be able to make an occasional drive-by in your region or even park in a hidden vantage point to stake-out a suspect area of a property.

If it seems that the warden doesn't appear to be spending much time focusing on your property, don't worry. Poachers typically "shine" many fields and croplands during a given night, methodically moving from one to another and, knowing this, the warden undoubtedly is patrolling the entire immediate area; if he doesn't apprehend the criminal on your particular land-holding but does indeed apprehend him a mile down the road on your neighbor's property, the problem is solved nonetheless.

If you see a spotlight panning fields or food plots, and want immediate results, especially if you hear shots, the agency to call is your local county sheriff's office. But don't simply report that someone is attempting to poach a deer; in these troubled times, that's generally a low-priority response matter. Instead, simply report that unknown individuals are on your property and you've heard gunfire, that will be treated as an urgent-response matter.

Also, of course, if an unfamiliar vehicle is occasionally seen cruising the county and township roads in your immediate area, and they're driving slowly and periodically stopping and doing a lot of "looking," their intentions probably are not in your best interests. So take the time to discreetly jot down the license plate number and vehicle description, in the event that it may give your law enforcement agency a solid lead if a criminal act is committed.

Avoid at all costs situating food plots that are clearly visible from nearby roads because they provide the easiest opportunities for poachers and other game-law violators.

This is where a concept known as QDM, which is fully discussed in the next chapter, plays an important role in the cooperative efforts of landowners who share adjoining property-lines. Don't simply be alert to the activities of no-gooders on your own property but on your neighbor's land as well. As a member of a local QDM co-operative, your neighbors will in turn be doing the same on your behalf.

In the case of daylight intruders attempting to hunt deer, turkeys, gamebirds, waterfowl or small game, the wisest course of action is to post your land to clearly proclaim it's private property and that trespassers and game-law violators will be prosecuted. And once again, strive to avoid personal confrontations; simply jot down the license numbers of any vehicles parked nearby and pass the information along to local authorities. As a bit of additional insurance, some landowners place a note on the vehicle's windshield, informing the owner that he's been trespassing on private property and his license number has been turned over to local authorities for their reference.

## DEALING WITH FOUR-LEGGED PREDATORS

A land manager also must continually deal with other critters, especially dogs and cats, which can decimate wildlife populations. Dogs will chase down and kill defenseless, newborn fawns at every opportunity, and they can just as easily kill adult deer in conditions of deep snow. Housecats easily destroy the nesting sites of rabbits, turkeys, gamebirds, waterfowl, and songbirds.

Rightfully, the blame shouldn't be placed upon the dogs and cats themselves—they're just following their natural animal instincts—but with their irresponsible owners who allow their pets to roam at large and inflict what damage they will, even on their neighbor's property. Unfortunately, it's usually futile to reason with individuals who refuse to control their pets, so it's often necessary to deal with the predators first-hand.

This is a touchy subject because over the years I myself have owned bird dogs, which I've always kept kenneled on my property when not hunting. Yet occasionally a dog would manage to get out and run loose for several hours before I became aware of its escape and could find the dog and return it to its kennel. If during the meanwhile the dog was shot while briefly roaming on an adjacent property, I would undoubtedly have been angered. So I can fully understand and appreciate one's feelings on either side of the fence, from both a wildlife manager's standpoint and from that of a pet owner.

Consequently, the policy I and most other wildlife managers now subscribe to, and which the reader should feel free to modify depending

Free-roaming dogs and cats can decimate wildlife populations. Wildlife managers must be mentally and emotionally prepared to deal with this situation, or be willing to suffer the losses.

upon his own perspective or other unique situation, involves the term "repetition."

What I mean is, if a free-roaming dog is occasionally spotted, and especially if it is a thoroughbred species and is wearing a collar, I give the animal the benefit of the doubt, even if it's seen chasing a deer. The dog's owner may, at that very moment, be driving the back roads in the vicinity looking for it. However, if the free-roaming dog is involved in repeatedly chasing deer, and is not a thoroughbred species and is not wearing a collar, and especially if the dog is packed-up with numerous others, I discreetly, with remorse, dispose of the animal(s).

Cats virtually never venture far from their homes to merely exercise a curiosity about their environments. So if you see a cat just once, it's a sound assumption it momentarily is on the loose and its owner is searching for it. However, if you see the cat repeatedly prowling about, and it's a good distance from its home, you can positively assume it's hunting.

It's been said by state wildlife departments that every year free-ranging cats kill more newborn rabbits, turkeys, gamebirds, common songbirds, rare songbirds, and endangered songbirds than most people ever suspect. So it's in wildlife's best interests to quickly, and as humanely as possible, deal with the problem when it becomes persistent.

This brings up the frequent question, "don't

Some predators such as bobcats are so few in number they pose little threat to a region's wildlife population. As part of the balance of nature, it's also nice having coyotes around but the land manager must remain vigilant to keep their numbers in check.

free-roaming dogs and cats play a role in predator-prey relationships with wildlife?" The answer is almost always "no," for the simple reason that free-roaming dogs and cats do not typically hunt in order to eat; they're usually well-fed by their owners. Rather, they hunt in order to satisfy their base instinct to kill, and once their prey has been killed it usually is abandoned as the dog or cat then resumes its search for yet another target of opportunity.

There are also other predators that can similarly be expected to be problematic at times. Coyotes, in particular, when hunting in packs numbering sometimes a half-dozen or more, can easily run-down deer in snow conditions. Otherwise, whether they're individuals or in packs, they're opportunists, taking an endless variety of game and non-game species.

We take coyotes randomly, merely to keep their numbers thinned out. But we don't want to eradicate them. Part of the relationship a steward of the land enjoys with wildlife is the balance of nature and the important role of legitimate predator-prey relationships that nature has intended. "Balance" is the key word here.

Bobcats also prey heavily upon turkeys and other birdlife, as well as small game, but in most regions their numbers are so low they're generally considered to be little threat.

Groundhogs are a two-pronged nuisance. They can devastate small clover and alfalfa food plots. And their mid-field burrowing of holes and tunnels, which often are hidden from view, can cause expensive damage to planting equipment.

There also are other four-legged predators a land manager may have to periodically contend with, but they don't always focus upon wildlife alone. Raccoons and possums readily come to mind. In the spring, both species eagerly invade nesting sites to eat the eggs of turkeys and gamebirds or kill new-born chicks. But the remainder of the year they focus their energies upon the wildlife manager's planting efforts. A half-dozen raccoons, for example, can decimate a tiny food plot of corn in just a few evenings.

Moreover, red and gray foxes can greatly reduce fruit-tree production, and they prey heavily upon small game, gamebirds, waterfowl, newly hatched turkey chicks, and songbirds.

Moreover, too many groundhogs and opossums can consume an unbelievable amount of clover, alfalfa, grain, and designer foods.

Controlling these predators is best accomplished through hunting and trapping activities. If you don't hunt or trap these species yourself, period-ically granting permission to others to do so is the most viable option.

Personally, I like seeing these latter critters around, as well, and I respect the role they play in nature's larger scheme. So I try to keep close tabs on their numbers by continually monitoring my food plots and the overall productivity levels of various wildlife populations. Then, at the very minute that I discover something is amiss, I make an assessment of the amount of damage that is occurring, and the specific animal species that is causing the detriment. Then and only then do I permit a modest amount of hunting or trapping activities among local, respected neighbors to remedy the problem.

# CHAPTER 18

## QUALITY
# DEER MANAGEMENT

None of us really ever own the land. We may be temporarily titled to it, but we're basically caretakers of it on behalf of the next generation. Unfortunately, there have been times in the past when we sometimes didn't do our job very well.

When I first began hunting, in my teens, it was a rather depressing endeavor. Most all game populations were at a very low level, due mostly to over-harvesting, poor management, and little enforcement of the game laws. But more than anything, few landowners did much on behalf of their wildlife populations. They looked upon game species as providing sport and food for the taking, and since it presumably was in endless supply there was no inclination to put anything back. Fortunately, our dress rehearsal is over, we've learned from it and slowly but steadily polished our act, and as a result "the good old days" are right now!

Largely, all of this is the result of having accepted the need to regularly put something back. Of course, you can't actually "put back" a deer or turkey taken for the table. But as we've seen in previous chapters, you can "put back" in terms of enhancing the habitat and carefully regulating the harvest to allow for high-quality, self-sustaining wildlife populations.

## INTRODUCING QDM

In recent decades, whitetail deer in particular have seen an almost miraculous comeback. Some might even say that in many regions we now have too many deer.

But mostly, they're in good balance with the available habitat and they're overall in excellent health. Moreover, in many regions, bucks now are growing larger antlers than previous generations only dreamed about. Much of this can be directly attributed to a concept known as Quality Deer Management. But most landowners just call it QDM, for short.

The concept of QDM is exhaustively outlined in the impressive textbook Quality Whitetails, published by the Quality Deer Management Association and compiled by noted University of Georgia deer biologists Karl Miller and Larry Marchinton. This reference book should be part of every wildlife manager's library, to be consulted often.

Of course, many land managers have long been looking after their deer simply by not harvesting the immature bucks, providing them with food and supplemental nutrients, and watching them steadily grow over the years to trophy proportions. It just seemed like the right thing to do and they didn't realize that one day a formal name would be given to the practice.

However, it should be emphasized that practitioners of Quality Deer Management don't narrow-mindedly focus upon mature bucks alone. QDM is a package deal in which a land manager strives for an overall healthy whitetail population of all age groups, and this includes the does and fawns as well. Also included in the QDM equation are viable habitat management practices that target deer but also are beneficial to other game and non-game species.

And finally, QDM promotes landowner relations. This is especially important because, no matter what size property you own or lease, your efforts in managing the deer and the acreage upon which they live will be infinitely more successful if your neighbors are cooperating by engaging in similar practices on their own land.

## MANAGING FOR TROPHY BUCKS

When it comes to managing for trophy whitetail bucks, we operated under many misconceptions for a long time. At one time, and this belief still prevails in certain regions, there was and still is the notion that "spike bucks are genetically inferior," and "once a spike, always a spike." But we now know those beliefs are myths and that given proper nutrition, and especially time, many spike bucks may eventually achieve so-called trophy status. Not all of them will, of course, because genetics do indeed play a role. But you won't really know which deer have the potential to achieve trophy status until they've been given time—usually, at least two or three years— to demonstrate their capabilities. Consequently, most educated land managers

**For more trophy bucks, forget about genetics and concentrate upon nutritional food plantings, vitamin and mineral supplements, and especially "time." You can't do much to control genetics, but you can grow big deer by letting the little bucks walk.**

nowadays abide by the rule of thumb to "let the little bucks walk."

But there's much more to it than that. In addition to providing deer with the best possible habitat and foraging opportunities, and giving young bucks the necessary time to prove themselves, the overall herd structure, in terms of its sex ratio, is critical to the vitality of the population.

In a perfect world, a 1:1 ratio (one doe to one buck) is the ideal-type. But this is a near-impossible goal, even for the most intensive land manager whose property is high-fenced. Nevertheless, if we know what the ideal-type is, and strive to achieve it, we're on the right track. And many of us come close by having deer populations in the range of 3 or 4 does for every buck; if a land manager can accomplish this on a tract of land that is not high-fenced, his efforts should be applauded.

Conversely, if does (both yearlings and adults) are not harvested in substantial numbers, the entire social structure of the herd can collapse. It begins with there not being enough mature bucks to breed the upward-spiraling doe population. When this happens, the breeding season becomes protracted—spread out over a longer time frame—with second and even third rutting periods taking place. And this, in turn, commonly results in the few mature bucks being overworked and overstressed to the extent that a percentage of them die that winter from a combination of weight loss and resulting pneumonia.

Meanwhile, the increasing doe population stresses the habitat itself because a given land-base has the capability of supporting only a given number of deer. Biologists can actually calculate all of this mathematically by using formulas representing how much tonnage of acceptable deer forage a land-base is producing annually in relation to how much tonnage of forage each inhabiting animal requires in that specific region. When the available forage-production falls below what the inhabiting deer population requires, and their reproductive rate continues upward, disaster is in the offing, with a large percentage of the population destined to perish.

## HOW QDM WORKS

QDM is the metaphorical first-aid kit that serves as the remedy. However, it won't work everywhere. It won't work in those pockets around the country where the local residents still cling to the false premise that it's necessary to protect the does by not harvesting them. And it won't work on those large tracts of public land that every year are subjected to intense hunting pressure; on these tracts of land, most hunters subscribe to the belief that if they don't shoot the first buck they see—no matter its age or the size of its rack—some other hunter a few hundred yards away will indeed take it.

As QDM spokesman Brian Murphy points out, "An ideal situation for quality managing of a deer herd is 1,000 contiguous acres of privately owned or leased land. Unfortunately, in these days and times, few among us can afford such a sizeable amount of acreage. And that's where still another tenet of QDM comes into play."

If a number of owners of relatively small parcels of land, preferably properties that share adjacent borders, pool their quality-deer-management beliefs and practices in a cooperative effort, the deer population, an especially the number of impressive trophy bucks in that specific region, can be expected to spiral upward!

Of course, achieving even this ideal-type is seldom possible because not all landowners in a given area are likely to be cooperative. So the situation typically results not in a solid block of well-defined QDM land but rather a patchwork quilt of properties that can best be described as a "QDM area" with spotty parcels not under deer management.

Nevertheless, the quality of the deer population enjoyed by any individual participating landowner can be dramatically improved by concentrating the

**Most land managers who are cooperatives in Quality Deer Management with their neighbors subscribe to two solid practices: They strive to remove from the land-base as many does as they're legally permitted to take; and, they take only those bucks that, minimally, have eight-point racks with a minimum-width spread of 16 inches.**

overall region's deer numbers in specific areas. And the way to do this, as we've seen in the many previous chapters, is for those QDM participants to put in food plots specifically targeting deer, providing other nutrients such as mineral licks, even engaging in supplemental feeding when necessary, and improving the habitat in numerous other ways. If they similarly engage in prescribed QDM harvesting recommendations, the quality of the hunting on two adjacent properties can be as different as day and night!

Of course, there is a good deal of latitude in the so-called "strictness" of a land-manager's QDM practices. I, for one, would never prohibit a youngster or other first-time hunter from taking an immature buck.

However, among seasoned hunters, a standard rule of thumb is that a buck must have antlers with a minimum of 8 points and a width-spread of at least 16 inches. Any hunter who is not too impulsive to get on with the matter of shooting can usually make these determinations quickly by simply taking a few moments to evaluate a given buck by first counting the points. Then he should pause long enough to study the width of the animal's rack; this is a relatively easy determination because a whitetail's ears, tip to tip, average 16 inches in width.

It can take three years of intelligent land-management practices, but if you're a serious believer in QDM and do all the right things, you'll eventually have bucks like this on your place.

## A LITTLE HELP FROM YOUR FRIENDS

The way to enlist the cooperation of individual neighboring landowners is to simply talk to them. Do this during the evening, at a time of year when they are not pressured with farming work. Better still, assemble several property owners for an informal group discussion of the benefits of beginning a cooperative QDM program. Even if all of them do not immediately begin putting in food plots specifically for deer, simply convincing them to make a few changes in their current deer-harvesting practices is a giant step in the right direction. Moreover, once several landowners are in agreement, it's much easier to gradually enlist growing numbers of others, one by one.

It's even worthwhile to consider not talking with neighbor landowners yourself but, instead, inviting someone else to speak to the group. Ideally, this should be a long-time QDM proponent who lives in the immediate area—someone who may even be known to those you've assembled—and have him describe first-hand how he and his neighbors formed a QDM cooperative and soon dramatically saw an increase in their trophy buck numbers.

## QDM RESOURCES

**Quality Deer Management Association**
P.O. Box 227
Watkinsville, GA 30677
(800) 209-3337
www.qdma.com

**Wildlife Management Institute**
Suite 801, 14th Street NW
Washington, DC 20005
(202) 371-1808
www.wildlifemgt.org